This book is dedicated to my mother, Marilyn H. Chase, a teacher and writer who has tirelessly encouraged countless students, as well as her own children, helping us all to discover those amazing places within our own imaginations that can calm us and free us.

—Robin K. Sprague

This book is also dedicated to the thousands of counselors and educators I have met over the last twenty-five years, who have helped so many children and so many parents.

—Lawrence E. Shapiro

The Relaxation & Stress Reduction Workbook for Kids

Help for Children to Cope with
Stress, Anxiety & Transitions

LAWRENCE E. SHAPIRO, PH.D.
ROBIN K. SPRAGUE, LCPC

Instant Help Books
A Division of New Harbinger Publications, Inc.

Publisher's Note

This publication is designed to provide accurate and authoritative information in regard to the subject matter covered. It is sold with the understanding that the publisher is not engaged in rendering psychological, financial, legal, or other professional services. If expert assistance or counseling is needed, the services of a competent professional should be sought.

Distributed in Canada by Raincoast Books

Copyright © 2009 by Lawrence E. Shapiro and Robin K. Sprague
        Instant Help Books
        A Division of New Harbinger Publications, Inc.
        5674 Shattuck Avenue
        Oakland, CA 94609
        www.newharbinger.com

Cover design by Amy Shoup
Illustrations done by Julie Olson

All photos are models used for illustrative purposes only.

Printed in the United States of America

Library of Congress Cataloging-in-Publication Data

Shapiro, Lawrence E.
 The relaxation and stress reduction workbook for kids : help for children to cope with stress, anxiety, and transitions / Lawrence E. Shapiro and Robin K. Sprague ; foreword by Matthew McKay.
   p. cm.
 Includes bibliographical references.
 ISBN-13: 978-1-57224-582-2 (pbk. : alk. paper)
 ISBN-10: 1-57224-582-4 (pbk. : alk. paper)
 ISBN-13: 978-1-57224-655-3 (pbk. + cd : alk. paper)
 ISBN-10: 1-57224-655-3 (pbk. + cd : alk. paper)
 1. Stress in children. 2. Anxiety in children. 3. Relaxation. I. Sprague, Robin K. II. Title.
 BF723.S75S53 2008
 155.4'18--dc22

                              2008039799

18   17   16

25   24   23   22   21   20   19   18   17   16   15

Table of Contents

Foreword

The Relaxation and Stress Reduction Workbook, 6th Edition (New Harbinger Publications, 2008) has helped over 900,000 people learn how to relax their bodies, calm their minds, and take control of their lives. The clinically proven stress management and relaxation techniques in that classic book help adults deal with stressful thoughts and feelings, manage time, and communicate more assertively, among many other things. When we first published *The Relaxation and Stress Reduction Workbook* over thirty years ago, we set out to create a resource that would help people relax so that they can do more of what matters to them.

In this new book, *The Relaxation and Stress Reduction Workbook for Kids*, authors Lawrence Shapiro and Robin Sprague provide the keys to reducing stress in your child's life. While some stress is normal and necessary for human development, too much can be harmful—to both you and your child. Financial problems, relationship problems, a death or illness in the family, fights with siblings, changing schools, even moving from one grade to the next can all be stressful transitions for you and your child. While you can't stop stressors from showing up, you can learn effective tools and techniques for dealing with them.

This book will help you pass these effective stress reduction tools on to your child. Offering activities that range from cultivating a peaceful home to learning to be a stress detective, these authors have created an invaluable resource that teaches parents and kids to effectively manage stress. This book includes some of the best relaxation strategies ever developed, including breathing, guided imagery, mindfulness, yoga, and even play, art, and laughter as doorways to relaxation and stress reduction. What I find so valuable about this book is the fun and creative ways it adapts proven techniques for kids. In just ten or fifteen minutes a day, you and your child will learn skills to last a lifetime.

There will always be stress, but this book shows you that there are healthy ways to manage it—and get more out of life. The skills in this book will help you and your child feel better *now*.

All the best,

Matthew McKay
coauthor of *The Relaxation and Stress Reduction Workbook, 6th Edition*

Acknowledgments

We wish to acknowledge Lynda McCann-Olson, accomplished elementary art teacher and artist, who shared her years of experience in helping develop the art exercises. We also wish to express a special thanks to Natalie Gregory and Christina Diebold for their tireless encouragement and helpful feedback in reviewing sections of the book.

Introduction for Parents

Stress is part of being human, and it begins even before birth. Think for a moment about a baby resting comfortably in his mother's uterus, when—bam!—labor begins. His world closes in with terrible force, and all of a sudden he is being pushed down the birth canal on a dark, claustrophobic journey. Finally he bursts out into the world, only to be met by lights, noise, and cold air and to be picked up, prodded, and wiped. What a welcome!

As this baby progresses through infancy and childhood, he will experience many joys, but he will also encounter much stress, and that's how it should be. Stress plays an important part in every stage of a child's development, from learning to hold his bottle to trying to master the multiplication tables. Every bit of learning and growth involves a degree of stress, followed by the indescribable pleasure of a new achievement.

But while a little stress is normal and healthful, too much stress isn't good at all. Significant stress—like that caused by starting a new school or having a family member with an illness—can have a profound effect on children. Even constant lower-level stress will take its toll. The effects can be physical, causing aches and pains and a host of health problems. Stress can also affect mood and behavior, making a child hyper, depressed, oppositional, or anxious. Most children will experience some emotional or behavioral problems as they grow, but stress makes everything worse.

Stress is not an abstract bogeyman, but a very real thing. We measure it by noting changes in the body: a rise in blood pressure, a change in metabolism and digestion, and a suppression of the immune system and the ability to heal. Stress causes the body to go on alert, putting a strain on virtually all its systems and creating an opportunity for diseases that might otherwise have been fought off.

But as you will read, stress reduction and relaxation make everything better. Teaching children to reduce stress will not only make every day happier, but may make the years to come healthier.

How to Use This Book

The first chapter in this workbook will help you reduce stress in your home. Doing this is not always easy, and it probably won't win you any popularity contests with your kids. You will have to turn off the TV more often and guide their eating habits more closely. You will need to get them to bed on time and out in the yard playing more often.

But the activities in Chapter 2 will make the job of stress reduction much easier, because your child will soon see that it is his job, too. Within a few days, we hope that you and your child will see that stress reduction is just another good health practice, like brushing your teeth or taking a bath.

Some types of stress will not readily go away. Your child may have a learning disability or a significant health problem, or perhaps there has been a change in the family: a divorce, a move, or a sick parent. These and many other situations will create stress for your child every day, but—and this is an important "but"—kids can learn simple and even fun ways to cope. The skills they will gain in this chapter will make even serious problems seem much easier to handle, and they will reduce the short- and long-terms effects of stress on your child's physical and mental health.

Chapters 3 through 9 of the book will help you and your child learn the importance of relaxation in dealing with stress. We are not talking about vegging out in front of the TV or even sleeping late on a Saturday morning, although catching up on sleep is not a bad idea. By "relaxation" we mean the active techniques that have become standard practice for most therapists and counselors in the country.

As you look through these chapters, you will find activities on breathing, guided imagery, mindfulness, yoga, using play to cope with stress, and more. All of these techniques will help your child learn to reduce the damaging effects of stress, but most children will find some techniques more appealing than others. We suggest you begin by looking through the book and reading about approaches that interest you. In our years of prescribing therapeutic activities to parents, we have found that the activities parents enjoy are the most effective for their children.

Once you find a type of relaxation that best fits you and your child—and possibly the rest of the family as well—there is one critical thing you must keep in mind. You must practice every day, because relaxation as a form of stress reduction is not a sometimes thing. As you will see, the relaxation activities in this workbook generally take just ten to fifteen minutes to do, but they will help your child only if you do them every day.

It is also worth noting that everything we are saying about children pertains to you as well. You will be happier and healthier if you reduce your own stress and take just ten minutes a day to practice relaxation.

So find a comfortable chair, turn on some quiet music, and take a few breaths from deep down in your lower belly. Relax your muscles. Close your eyes for a few minutes and imagine that you are sitting on a dock overlooking a placid lake and that the cool breeze has brought you calm and comfort. We bet you feel better already! And if not … well, start reading Chapter 1.

Best of luck on your journey,

The Authors

Chapter 1
Reducing Stress in Your Home

Even though you bought this workbook for your child, this chapter is just for you, because you are the biggest influence in reducing stress in your home. Whatever causes of stress are affecting your family—financial problems, marital problems, illness, moving your household—the steps you will take in this chapter will make a difference.

If you are ready to help reduce the stress in your child's life, the best place to start is with yourself. The chapter begins with activities that will help you look at your own stress and consider what you can do about it. You will then look at some of things in your home that you may take for granted but in fact are adding stress for you and your child. Do you both live a healthy lifestyle? Does your parenting style make life easier or harder for your child? Is too much technology increasing the stress in your home?

Many parents tell us that they often feel overwhelmed by life's demands, as if they were being pulled in six directions at once. But life doesn't have to be that way. There will always be stress, but there are many things you can do to make it more manageable. The activities in this chapter will get you started, and the activities in the rest of the workbook can benefit you as well as your child.

If you feel like you need some extra help, please get it. People with a lot of stress will benefit from seeing a professional therapist who can not only help them with stress-reduction techniques, but can also teach them better ways to cope with stress. The best way to find a therapist is through recommendation, but several online services, such as www.Find-a-Therapist.com and www.PsychologyToday.com, also provide therapy referrals.

Just How Stressed Are You?

Do you recall what flight attendants tell you to do if there is a loss of cabin pressure and the oxygen masks descend? "Put on your own oxygen mask, then help your child." The same is true when it comes to dealing with stress. Think about what you can do to reduce stress in your own life before you do the same for your child.

While everyone has some stress, there is no question that some people simply have more than others, and it is helpful to recognize your stressful areas so that you can do something about them. Just like going to a doctor for a physical, let's begin with a checkup by taking stock of the things that cause you stress.

On the following chart, we've listed typical areas of stress that parents face: work issues, family problems, health issues, and so on. You'll rate each area on a 3-point scale and then add up your score. Thirty-nine is the highest possible score.

If you score in the 0–13 range, you have a mild amount of stress. If your score is 14–26, you have a moderate amount of stress. You are approaching the danger zone, but we hope that using this book with your child will also help you learn ways to cope with your own stress. If your score is 27–39, you need to understand that stress is a serious threat to your health. You likely need some extra support from a counselor, member of the clergy, or a close family member or friend. We urge you to make your health a priority for your sake and the sake of your family.

Parent's Stress Test

Circle the statements in each column that apply to you. If a particular area of your life doesn't generally cause you stress, skip it.

Cause of stress	Mild (1 point)	Moderate (2 points)	Serious (3 points)
Work	I work part-time.	I work full-time.	I work more than forty hours a week.
Number of kids	One	Two	Three or more
Parents	My parents occasionally need my help.	My parents have chronic problems and need my help more and more.	My parents live with me because of chronic problems.
In-laws	My in-laws occasionally need my help.	My in-laws have chronic problems and need my help more and more.	My in-laws live with me because of chronic problems.
Health	I have typical complaints for my age.	I have mild health problems.	I have moderate to severe health problems.
Finances	I manage to save a little but not much.	I am often worried that we don't have enough money.	I have serious financial problems.
Weather	I experience seasonal problems, such as long winters.	I experience severe weather problems, like hurricanes and tornadoes.	My home has been affected by a weather-related disaster.
Space	We are crowded at home.	We have just barely enough space at home.	We have fights over space every week.
Commuting	I commute less than a half hour a day.	I commute from a half hour to an hour a day.	I commute more than one hour a day.

The Relaxation & Stress Reduction Workbook for Kids

Support system	I have some friends and family nearby but not enough.	I have family and friends, but most are not nearby.	I have almost no one I can talk to or get support from.
Kids' problems	My kids have normal problems with friends and at school.	My kids have moderate problems that affect their happiness.	My kids have serious learning, physical health, or mental health problems.
Neighborhood	It could be better.	It's marginal.	It's not safe.
Other problems at home	I have occasional other problems at home.	I have frequent other problems at home.	I have multiple problems at home that never seem to get better.
Total			

Finding Ways to
Reduce Stress

Now that you have some idea of how stressed you are, we'd like you to think about what you can do to help yourself cope. The following activities can help you reduce stress (as can many of the other activities in this workbook). Check off the ones you already do on a regular basis. Put a star next to the ones you don't do, but can begin to do very soon, perhaps today or tomorrow. These are simple ways to make a real difference in your life. Don't put them off.

- ☐ Exercise daily for at least a half hour.

- ☐ Talk to friends.

- ☐ Read a book.

- ☐ Practice yoga or meditation.

- ☐ Get a massage.

- ☐ Do crafts or hobbies.

- ☐ Garden.

- ☐ Take a long walk.

- ☐ Listen to relaxing music.

- ☐ Participate in clubs or social groups.

- ☐ Eat healthily.

- ☐ Cut down on caffeine and alcohol.

There are also simple, common activities that will help you reduce stress in your family. Check off the activities that you do with your family on a regular basis. Put a star next to the ones that you don't all do now, but can do this week.

- ☐ Eat dinner together.

- ☐ Have family meetings.

- ☐ Attend religious services as a family.

☐ Spend time with extended-family members.

☐ Participate in family sports.

☐ Play board games and other indoor games.

☐ Enjoy nature activities.

☐ Take a nonstressful trip.

☐ Go on a picnic.

☐ Listen to music together.

☐ Have a movie night.

Do you have other ideas for you or your family? Write them below.

_____

_____

_____

_____

_____

Activity 3   Setting Clear Limits

We all like to see our children happy, but permissive parenting—buying them anything their hearts desire, giving them the fast food they crave, letting them stay up late—does more harm than good. Saying no to children may not feel good, but "no" is a word children need to hear. In fact, studies tell us that when kids don't hear it enough, when they have few limits to their actions, they actually experience more stress.

Children need limits. They need to eat healthy food. They need to have the TV turned off and to be sent out to play. They need to get to sleep on time. They need to have chores and other responsibilities around the home. When you set clear limits for your children and enforce them consistently, you will be creating less stress for everyone in the home.

One of the simplest ways to set clear limits is through a behavioral contract. Use the chart on the next page to clarify the rules of the house. You will need one chart for each child.

> For more complete behavioral tools, check out www.Handipoints.com. This well-thought-out website helps you create behavioral charts, and your children can earn points toward no-cost rewards they can use in a fun, virtual world.

The Rules in Our House

We _____ (parents' names)

and _____ (child's name) agree to the following household rules:

Bedtime is _____.

Your chores will be _____, _____,

and _____.

You will improve your eating habits by trying _____

and not eating _____.

You will spend not more than _____ watching TV.

Other rules:

_____

_____

_____

We make rules because we love you.

Your Parents _____
(signatures)

Child _____
(signature)

Activity 4   Too Much Technology

For many people, the American dream is all about technology: a big-screen TV in the living room, a cell phone and MP3 player for every family member, computers and high-speed Internet everywhere we go. While technology can be fun, many families, and particularly many kids, are overexposed to gadgets and gizmos that cause unnecessary and unhealthy stress.

There are many reasons why technology takes a toll on our psyches:

- Loud noises are a significant stress.

- Technology tends to cut us off from interacting with other people.

- Multitasking discourages concentration and awareness of our environment.

- We spend too much time in sedentary indoor activities when our bodies need exercise and fresh air.

You can reduce the stress in your home by putting family members (yes, you and your spouse, too) on a technology diet. Studies tell us that kids spend an average of three hours a day in front of a TV or computer screen. Can you cut that in half?

To help, make a copy of the following form for everyone in the house. Begin by having family members keep track of the time they spend in front of a screen for entertainment for one week. Then for the second week, have family members compete to reduce their times by reading, exercising, doing a hobby, and so on. At the end of the week, talk about how it went and see if you can reduce this unnatural stress for good.

> *Note*: Time at a computer for homework or necessary adult work should not be counted. However, as an adult, consider whether you really need to bring your work home, particularly when your children are around. Working around the clock is a stress on you and your children.

My Technology Log

Name _____ Week of _____

Enter the minutes for each time you are in front of a screen for entertainment purposes, including TV, computer games, Web surfing, and video games.

Activity	Mon	Tues	Wed	Thurs	Fri	Sat	Sun
Total							

Activity 5   Creating a Peaceful Home

Think back to your own childhood for a moment. What are the five most stressful moments that come to mind? If you are like many adults, family fights are at the top of your list.

All couples argue at some time. All kids lose their tempers, too. It is rare to find siblings who don't occasionally quarrel or call each other names. But arguing and fighting should be an exception, not a rule. If your family life is tainted by constant bickering, sarcasm, yelling, or other forms of arguing, you should put peacemaking at the top of your stress-reduction to-do list.

> *Note:* Child and spousal abuse is a widespread problem. Any form of physical abuse in the family, even a single incident, is cause for intervention. If abuse is happening in your home, you can be immediately referred to a domestic violence hotline by calling 800-799-7233.

Everyone, even children as young as five, can learn peacemaking or conflict-resolution skills. Conflict-resolution programs have been used in schools for more than a decade, and there is one thing we know about them: they work. There are many ways to teach these same skills at home. Here is one activity that can help family members find peaceful ways to resolve their differences.

The Complaint-Box Game

You'll need a shoe box or other box with a lid, a marker, scissors, paper, and pencils.

1. Label the box top "Complaint Box," and cut a slot in it.

2. Ask any family member who has a problem with another person in the family to write it on a piece of paper and put the paper in the box. Younger children can dictate their complaints.

3. Once a week at a designated time, gather the family together to review the complaints in the box.

4. Problems often resolve themselves, but if a problem still exists, give the person who wrote the complaint two minutes to talk about it. During that time, no one may interrupt.

5. Ask all family members (including the person making the complaint) to write down two or more ways to resolve the complaint, and then read these ideas out loud.

6. The person making the complaint then decides which solution (including his or her own) is the most positive. The person who came up with that solution gets a point.

7. Continue for twenty minutes, or until all the complaints in the box have been resolved. If there are complaints left in the box after twenty minutes, play the game again the next day.

8. The person with the most points becomes the peacemaker for the week and may get a small prize or extra privilege for being so smart.

This activity will probably not transform your family overnight, but it is a start. Here are some other resources you might consider to help create a more peaceful home:

1. Practice active and respectful listening. See *How to Talk So Kids Will Listen & Listen So Kids Will Talk*, by Adele Faber and Elaine Mazlish (1999, Collins Living).

2. Play cooperative games with your family. See Dale LeFevre's *New Games for the Whole Family* (1988, Perigee Trade).

3. Teach your children the importance of empathy and concern for others. See *Learning to Listen, Learning to Care* by Lawrence E. Shapiro (2008, Instant Help Books).

If you feel that your family problems have gotten to a point where your input is not enough, seek help from a qualified family therapist or counselor.

Chapter 2
Don't Let Stress Get You Down

In Chapter 1, you learned about things you can do to reduce the stress in your child's life and in yours. In this chapter, your child will learn how to reduce her own stress and to cope in positive ways with stressful situations that can't be changed.

The activities will help your child recognize the big and little things that can cause her stress and will give her ideas about what can be done to make stress reduction a daily habit. Your child will also learn how a healthy lifestyle—eating right, exercising, getting enough sleep, and not spending too much time in front of the TV or computer—helps make it easier to cope with stress.

Some children seem to be born with resiliency skills that enable them to bounce back from almost every adversity. Others seem to be overwhelmed by problems and may take a passive attitude, feeling that there is nothing they can do to improve their situations; these children are more prone to react to stress with anger, worry, sadness, or even health problems. Still others react to stress with self-defeating behaviors. They may stop doing schoolwork; they may participate in high-risk behaviors; they may get into fights with kids, and even adults.

The good news is that children can learn resiliency skills that will make it much easier for them to cope with stress. The activities in this chapter will teach them:

- The importance of talking about their feelings

- How talking to themselves (self-talk) can combat stress

- How to solve problems rather than letting them continue

- How a positive, optimistic attitude can help reduce stress

As you work with your child on these activities, you may be tempted to ask a lot of questions, particularly if your child tells you about problems you weren't aware of. Resist that temptation. As child therapists, we have worked with hundreds of children over the years, and we know categorically that children do not respond well to direct questions of this type. Instead, work alongside your child as she does the activities in this section and throughout the book. Feel free to make nonjudgmental comments like, "That must be hard for you" or "I wonder what that feels like." You can also tell your child what you see when you look at her. You might say something like, "You really look worried when you talk about that" or be even more specific and say, "You look so tense. Your hands are balled up in tight fists." As you can see, making nonjudgmental statements is very different from asking direct questions, and it is the best way to support your child's emotional development and coping skills.

Being a good role model is also important in teaching your child about stress reduction. If you don't live a healthy lifestyle—if you eat the wrong things, avoid exercise, or don't get enough sleep—you certainly can't expect your child to act differently. If you react to stress in your life by yelling or drinking alcohol or getting depressed, think of what you are teaching your child. And if you don't take time to relax and take care of yourself, how do you expect your child to do this?

So as you go through the activities in the rest of the book, think of yourself as well as your child. The serious effects of stress are the same for children and adults, and stress reduction and relaxation activities will work the same way on both your child and you.

Do you know what *stress* means? It means putting extreme or constant pressure on someone or something. When you are pressured like that, your brain triggers the release of chemicals that give you a quick boost of energy to help you deal with whatever is causing you stress.

Your brain produces these energy-boosting chemicals for some very good reasons. If you were attacked by a lion in the jungle, you would need your energy to run away—but that probably won't happen too often! If someone makes fun of you, you need energy to make a good decision about what to do. You may think that you should fight this person (and you would need energy to do that), but you can probably think of something better to do than fighting. Fighting, even if you win, will just bring more stress. If you have a test at school, you probably feel stress. In this case, the extra energy your brain produces will help you do well on your test.

But when you have lots and lots of stress, these energy-boosting chemicals don't help you anymore, and they can even start to get you sick. When kids are under lots of stress, they worry a lot. They may need to go to the bathroom more often than usual and they may have stomachaches or headaches. They may even have problems thinking clearly.

You may have heard adults talk about feeling stressed. They might complain about having to pay bills or go to a job they don't like, or they might just complain about growing older. But kids have stress, too. In fact, kids have much more stress than most adults realize. Here are some of the big things that cause kids stress:

- Parents having problems

- Fighting with a friend or a sibling

- Taking a test

- Not having enough privacy

- Moving to a new school

- A parent getting married again

- Not having enough money

- Problems with teachers

- A new baby in the family

Do you have any of these big stresses? Circle them in red. Next, write down any other big stresses you have:

_____

_____

_____

_____

_____

Little things can cause stress, too. Here are some of the little things that cause kids stress:

- Having pimples

- Being sick

- Having homework

- Having too many chores

- Changes in their bodies as they become teenagers

- Hard schoolwork

- Wondering if someone likes them

- A brother or sister who is a pain in the neck

Circle any of these stresses that you have and write down any other little stresses here:

_____

_____

_____

_____

_____

How stressed are you? It probably changes from day to day. Make a copy of the Stress Scale that follows, and carry it with you. At the end of the day, circle the face that best describes how stressed you were that day. Then, on a calendar, write the number (from 1 to 7) that shows how stressed you felt. Do this every day for a month and see if using this workbook can keep your number at 5 or above, or even eliminate your stress entirely.

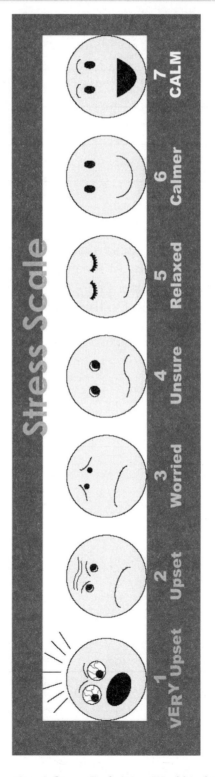

You certainly can't eliminate all the stress from your life, and there are some kinds of stress that you just have to learn to live with. But reducing stress even just a little bit will help you feel better.

The form that follows will help you be a stress detective. You can use it to find out what things cause you stress and what can be done about them. You should complete this form with a grown-up who may know some stresses in your life that you aren't even aware of.

The last column on the chart is the most important. There you'll write down simple things you can do to reduce your stress. This book will teach you lots of ways to cope with stress, but sometimes just little things can make a difference. Here are some ideas. Circle any ones that you think can help you:

- Take a walk.

- Call a friend.

- Listen to some quiet music.

- Distract yourself by doing something fun.

- Read a good book.

- Watch a good movie.

- Go for a swim.

Add other simple things you can do:

_____

_____

_____

_____

Be a Stress Detective

Thing that causes stress	Time of day it occurs*	Simple things you can do to reduce this stress

* It's important to be aware of the time of day stress occurs. You may find that some tasks that cause stress at one time can be done at other times instead. You may also notice that certain times of day are usually more stressful for you. At those times, you should pay more attention to stress reduction.

Where Do You Feel Stress?

Your body doesn't like stress, and it wants you to know it! Some people get stomachaches when they feel stressed, and others get headaches. Stress can also trigger asthma, rashes, sweaty palms, and a dry mouth. Stress makes it hard for some people to poop, and it makes others have to poop all the time—and neither is much fun!

In the outline below, color the places where you are most likely to feel stress. If you feel stress in your body a lot of the time, some of the activities in Chapter 4 can help.

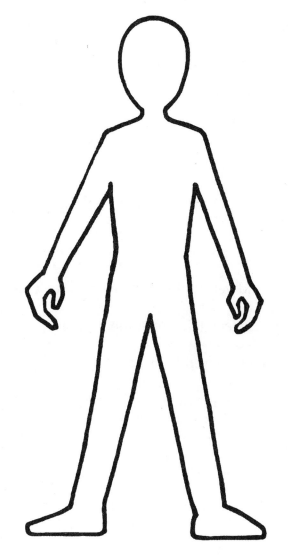

Help for Children to Cope with Stress, Anxiety & Transitions

Activity 9

Having a Healthy Lifestyle

There are lots of things that can cause you stress, like having too much homework or too many things to do in a day or trying out for a team you really want to make. You probably already know that these things can be stressful because they cause you to feel upset or worried or unhappy.

But did you know that even things you enjoy can be stressful? For example, all of these things cause your body stress, too, even if it doesn't seem that way:

- Loud music

- TV

- Violent video games

- Junk food

- Not getting enough sleep

- Lying around on the couch

Having a healthy lifestyle will reduce your stress. That means:

- Eating lots of fruits and vegetables and not too much sugar

- Getting a good night's sleep (eight or nine hours)

- Getting at least an hour of exercise a day

- Limiting the time you spend watching TV and playing computer or video games to no more than two hours a day

The Relaxation & Stress Reduction Workbook for Kids

Having a Healthy Lifestyle

Having a healthy lifestyle can be harder than people think, but it will be easier if you set goals for yourself. Fill in the following sentences below and try to meet these goals in the next few weeks.

I will improve my diet by eating more _____

and less _____.

I will _____ so that I can sleep better.

I will get more exercise by _____ almost every day.

I will _____

instead of watching TV and playing computer or video games.

Activity 10   Talking About Your Feelings

Everyone has dozens of different feelings every day. In just one day, you may be happy, sad, angry, fearful, proud, surprised, guilty, worried, thoughtful, bored, and excited—and that's just the beginning!

When you are stressed, you tend to pay more attention to your negative feelings. You may be more angry than usual or more sad than usual. You will almost always feel more worried and anxious. Being under a lot of stress doesn't erase your positive feelings, so you can still be proud and happy and peaceful. But stress may make it hard for you to pay attention to those positive feelings.

Here is a game that will help you talk about your feelings. Talking about your feelings, whether they are positive feelings or ones that are difficult for you, will always make you feel better.

Feelings Penny Pitch

You'll need six pennies, a timer, and the Feelings Target on the next page.

1. Take turns with another player and pitch a penny onto the target.

2. Wherever the penny lands, talk about the last time that you had that feeling. Talk for at least one minute.

3. If a penny lands between two feelings, you can talk about either feeling. Move the penny on top of the feeling that you are talking about.

4. After each player has taken three turns, do one of the relaxation activities in this book.

Feelings Target

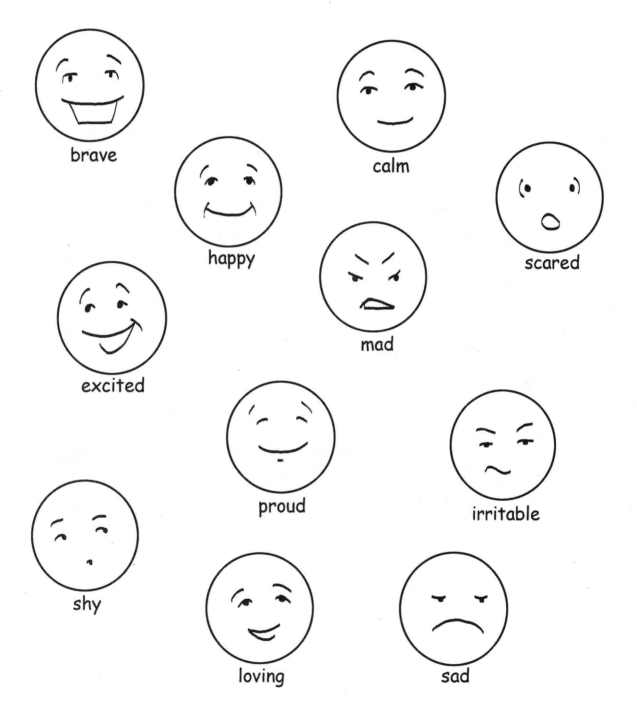

Help for Children to Cope with Stress, Anxiety & Transitions

Activity 11   Talking to Yourself

If you saw someone walking down the street talking to herself, you would probably think she was talking on a cell phone. If you noticed that she didn't have a phone, then you might just think she was a little weird. But talking to yourself (not out loud, just in your mind) is actually another good way to reduce stress.

When you are stressed, you probably feel tired and discouraged. But you can give yourself a pep talk, just like a coach who wants players to try a little harder. Here are some things you could say to yourself:

- I did my best, and that is good enough.

- If I keep trying, things will improve.

- I won't let this bother me.

- Practice makes perfect.

- I'm almost done, and I can keep going.

On the next page, write down some other things you could say to yourself that would help you deal better with stress. Make a copy of your "Things I Need to Know" page, and place it somewhere you will see it every day. Practice saying these things to yourself over and over again for five minutes every day. Talking to yourself like this may seem strange at first, but it will really help reduce your stress.

Things I Need to Know

Activity 12

The Brainstorming Game

Robert couldn't stand going to school. He had a hard time reading, and he didn't want anyone to know about it. Sometimes when he was supposed to read out loud, Robert would get a stomachache and he would be sent to the school nurse.

Jamie's parents were getting a divorce, and she didn't like going to see her dad every other weekend. She wanted to be with her friends on the weekends, but that was impossible when she was at her dad's house because he lived so far away. Jamie decided that she just wouldn't talk to her dad when she was there, and that would make him not want her around.

Kyra was always by herself at school. She didn't know why the other girls didn't seem to like her, but they just didn't. Kyra cried herself to sleep almost every night. She would cry very softly so her parents wouldn't hear her and be worried.

Do you know what these three kids have in common? They all have problems that cause them stress, but none of them has found a good solution. In fact, the solutions they have come up with will probably just make things worse.

Robert, Jamie, and Kyra are like a lot of kids, and a lot of adults, too. They think of one way to handle a stressful problem, but they don't see that there are many ways to handle the same problem. Some of these ways are better than others.

The game that follows will teach you how to come up with a different way to approach problems that cause you stress. This approach is called *brainstorming*. It is a way to be creative, to let your brain totally loose to come up with as many ideas as you can. When you brainstorm, there are no right or wrong ideas.

The Brainstorming Game

You'll need a trash can, paper, pencils, and a timer.

1. Find at least one other person to play with you.

2. Put the trash can in front of all the players.

3. Give each player a pencil and a piece of paper.

4. Set the timer for five minutes.

5. Within the five-minute period, players should write down as many things as they can think of to do with a trash can, other than using it for trash. The things don't have to be practical or even make any sense. The point is just to come up with lots of ideas.

6. The person who comes up with the most ideas is the winner!

Now you know how brainstorming works. Whenever you feel like giving your imagination some exercise, just play this game. You can use any common object, like a toothbrush, a frying pan, or a ball of string.

But the real challenge is in brainstorming solutions to the problems that cause you stress. On the Brainstorming Activity Sheet that follows, write down one problem that is causing you lots of stress. Take five minutes to think of all the solutions to the problem that you can. See how many you come up with. You might invite someone to help you, because two people working together can usually come up with more ideas.

Brainstorming Activity Sheet

My problem is _____.

The solutions I brainstormed are:

_____

_____

_____

_____

_____

_____

_____

_____

_____

_____

Now go back and circle the solutions you think are the best ones. Of the ones you circled, put 1, 2, or 3 next to the three best solutions.

The next step is to try them. If your best solution doesn't work, try the next best one, and so on. If none of them work, go back and play the brainstorming game.

Optimist or Pessimist? Activity 13

Some people have negative attitudes and think that bad things will keep happening. Others have positive attitudes and think that things will get better. We call people who have a negative attitude *pessimists,* and people who have a positive attitude are called *optimists.* Which one are you?

Circle the following statements that describe how you feel about your life.

1. My life stinks.

2. I'm having some problems now, but they will soon get better.

3. No one listens to me.

4. I know that lots of people have more problems than I do.

5. My parents don't understand me.

6. When I have a problem, I know my parents will help me.

7. I don't think my problems will ever go away.

8. People come to me for help when they have problems.

9. Nobody really likes me; even my friends treat me badly sometimes.

10. I have lots of friends and I like meeting new people.

Now go back and look at the statements that you circled. The statements with the odd numbers are thoughts that a pessimistic person often has. The statements with the even numbers are thoughts that are more typical of an optimist.

Activity 13

Optimist or Pessimist?

Do you know why it is better to be an optimist than a pessimist? There are lots of reasons. Optimists usually have more friends. They have fewer emotional problems and are depressed less often. They are happier with themselves and their lives. And here is the big one: optimists are better at handling stress.

Scientists tell us that people are either born optimists or pessimists. But they also tell us that if you were born a pessimist, you can change the way you think. See if you can do it. On the next page, you'll find a Thought-Changing Machine. Negative thoughts go in one side, and positive thoughts come out the other. Write down ten negative thoughts that you have about yourself or your life, and see if you can change them into ten positive thoughts.

The Relaxation & Stress Reduction Workbook for Kids

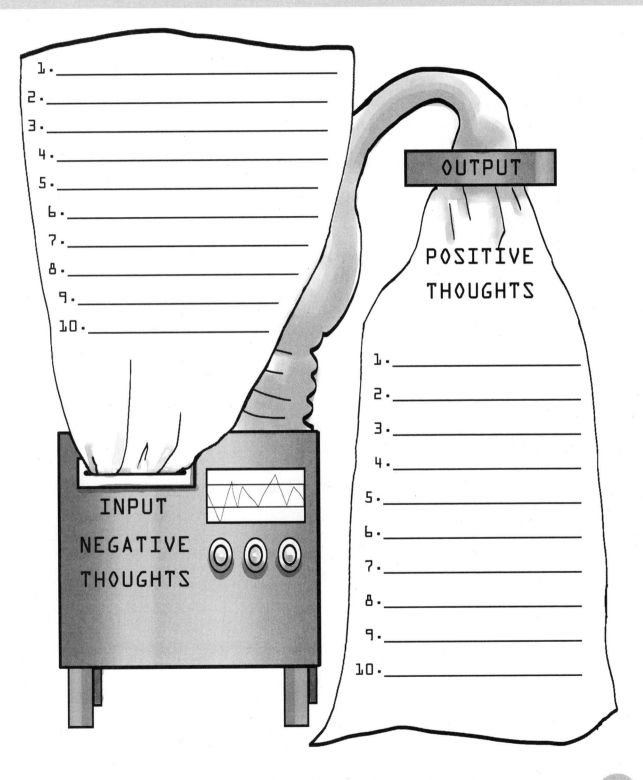

Activity 14　　　An Attitude of Gratitude

Some people believe that thinking more positively not only makes us feel better but actually helps change our lives. We know that we feel happier when we focus on things that we are thankful for and things that are going right.

Even when you feel like everything is going wrong, you can always find something that is going right. Tell yourself that the feeling of everything being wrong is not the whole truth. Talk back to those negative thoughts and tell them you are going to find things that are going right.

Here is an experiment: For two days, try smiling and saying thanks to your mom and dad at least six times a day when they do something for you. Tell them you appreciate what they do. Give them hugs. Be a detective and see if their attitudes change. Notice how it feels to practice being grateful. Practice it at school, too. Practice with your sister or brother, if you have one. (This might be harder, but try!)

If you notice that you feel happier, add this to your experiment: Every night right before you go to sleep, think of ten things you are grateful for. If something went well that day because of you, include that, too. If your mom or dad has time to listen to you say your list out loud, that's great. If not, say it to yourself. The more you do it, the easier it will get. We bet it will be a piece of cake for you to name ten things.

We hope your attitude-of-gratitude experiment brings lots of happy feelings into your life.

A Note to Parents

If you think your child is a negative pessimistic thinker, you will probably want to pay some extra attention to this problem. It is well worth the time. Refer to *The Optimistic Child* (2007, Houghton Mifflin) by Dr. Martin Seligman, the founder of the Penn Resiliency Project at the University of Pennsylvania. You may also want to check out www.Fishfulthinking.com, a website that promotes optimistic thinking as a way to improve mental health. You'll find lots of activities and information for kids, parents, and teachers on this site.

Chapter 3
Correct Breathing: A Key to Relaxation

Just hold your breath for sixty seconds and you'll be reminded about the importance of breathing. Every cell in your body needs oxygen every minute of the day. It provides the energy you need to metabolize food, break down waste products and toxins, build up your immune system, and much more. Deprived of oxygen, your brain will quickly start to call it quits.

The way you breathe also makes a big difference to your body. Expectant mothers are taught to take short, shallow breaths during labor, because this helps them focus on the job at hand rather than on the pain. Athletes take deep, steady breaths to increase endurance. Singers need to make sure that sufficient air passes through the larynx to maintain pure quality of sound, and the air flow must be adjusted to minimize the vibration of their vocal cords.

Relaxation also requires a specific breathing technique called *diaphragmatic breathing* (we'll call it *belly breathing* when explaining it to kids), which you and your child can learn to do. No single tool is more effective for calming the body and the brain than diaphragmatic breathing.

Scientists have found that stress causes us to take rapid and shallow breaths that come from the mid- to upper chest. While this type of breathing gives us a quick energy boost and can help us focus our attention, it also reduces the efficiency of our metabolism and interferes with our natural healing systems. This is why prolonged stress can be so damaging.

The connection between diaphragmatic breathing and stress reduction is not a recent discovery. The practice of focused breathing as a tool for meditation and relaxation comes down to us through centuries and across many diverse cultures; modern science has simply confirmed ancient wisdom.

Give Belly Breathing a Try

Before you can teach your child how to use breathing to relax, you must first learn this technique yourself. Diaphragmatic breathing involves breathing slowly and deeply from your belly instead of your chest while keeping your attention focused about two inches below your belly button. Focusing your attention on your belly as it rises and falls is both centering and calming.

As you breathe, try to keep a continuous flow of air without thinking about the beginning or end of each breath. Pay attention only to the feeling of the breath. If other thoughts wander in, just let them wander out again.

To teach belly breathing to your child, begin with the suggested language below, or a similar explanation in your own words. Tell your child that learning belly breathing is simple and fun, even though it may not seem natural at first.

Basic Belly Breathing

First have your child sit comfortably with his legs uncrossed. Say something like this:

"We're going to spend a couple of minutes playing a breathing game. Just put your hands on your belly a couple of inches below your belly button. Let your eyes close. That's good. Imagine a smile on your face, whether you have one or not. Be aware of how your belly rises and falls as you slowly breathe in and out. Now let your breathing get even slower, and I'll count 'one … two … three' as you breathe in and 'one … two … three' as you breathe out."

Continue counting while your child breathes this way for one to three minutes. The counting is not as important as having your child notice the feeling of his breath coming in and going out. Afterward, ask your child what it felt like. Did he feel more relaxed when he did his belly breathing?

If your child has trouble getting the hang of belly breathing, suggest that he lie down and put a favorite small toy or stuffed animal on his belly. Ask him to put all his attention into making the toy go up and down with his breathing. If he resists practicing, you might give him stickers or some small prize to reinforce the game. Once you have introduced belly breathing to your child, you may want to guide him through some of the other breathing games in this section. Each one has a different purpose, so try them all.

As with other many other relaxation techniques, the effect of belly breathing is enhanced when it is accompanied by soft, relaxing music. Classical music is fine, or you can also find many albums or music downloads specifically made to help people relax.

The most important thing to remember is to make time for belly breathing, along with other relaxation techniques you'll learn about in this book, every day. No matter what type of relaxation technique you practice with your child, it is a good idea to start with a few minutes of belly breathing.

Making time for relaxation means setting aside ten or fifteen minutes every day, finding a comfortable place to practice relaxation, and getting rid of all distractions. Turn off your cell phone. Tell the rest of your family you are taking a relaxation break and should not be interrupted, or alternatively, invite them to join you. Just concentrate on the pleasurable task at hand: helping your child relax and relaxing yourself, too.

The Relaxation & Stress Reduction Workbook for Kids

Spell Your Name with Belly Breaths

Now that you know how to breathe from your belly, here is another way to practice.

Lie down, or sit comfortably with your feet on the floor, and close your eyes. Let your hands rest a couple of inches below your belly button.

Take three long, deep breaths. Feel yourself relaxing more and more with each breath. Pay attention to how your breath feels going in and out.

With every out-breath, say to yourself (silently) one letter of your first name. For example, let's say your name is Mark. Breathe in, then breathe out and silently say "M." Breathe in again, and as you breathe out, silently say "A." Do the same with "R" and "K." Keep going until you've spelled your whole name.

After you've finished, ask yourself how you feel. If you are still stressed, start over or go on to your last name. If your name is a long one, like Passagassawakeag or Gookenburger-Pickleheim, it could take a while, but that's okay!

Can you think of a time that relaxing with belly breathing might be really important? Do you get stressed when you are taking a test? Do you sit next to someone at school who is really annoying? How about when you have to get a cavity filled in the dentist's office?

Think of five situations where you feel really stressed and belly breathing might help. Write them here:

_____

_____

_____

_____

_____

Activity 16   How Great I Am

Here is another belly-breathing game that will also remind you how special you are.

Lie on your back or sit comfortably with your feet on the floor. Let your hands rest a little below your belly button, and just let your eyes close. Feel your belly rise and fall as you breathe in and out. Now breathe in slowly to the count of three, and let your breath out just as slowly: one … two … three.

As you breathe, feel yourself relaxing more and more with each breath. Feel your muscles relax. Say to yourself, "I am relaxed." Say this two or three times.

Now here is the really important part. As you breathe in, say silently to yourself "I am…." As you breathe out, complete the sentence with the word "peaceful."

Breathe in again and say, "I am…." Breathe out and complete the sentence with the word "wonderful."

Continue doing this, saying special words that describe how great you are every time you breathe out, such as:

"I am … brave."

"I am … kind."

"I am … a loving friend."

On the lines below, write five special words or short sentences that describe you, and use them with this belly-breathing game.

1. _____

2. _____

3. _____

4. _____

5. _____

The Relaxation & Stress Reduction Workbook for Kids

Make a list of some favorite things or places or people that always make you feel really good. Here are some ideas:

- Your grandma hugging you

- Patting your dog

- Being with your best friend

- Playing with your favorite toy

Make a copy of the next page and write your favorite things on it. Then put it in a place where you will see it many times during the day, like on the refrigerator or in a notebook.

When you are feeling stressed, take three long belly breaths, feeling yourself relax more with each breath. Then choose something from your list to focus on. Try to see it in your mind's eye. Try to hear what might be going on. Can you smell the smells? Can you feel what is happening as if you were really there? Try this for a couple of minutes while you do your belly breathing, and see what happens.

My Favorite Things

The Relaxation & Stress Reduction Workbook for Kids

Breathing Happy Thoughts

Do you ever wish you could change your feelings? Do you ever wish that you wouldn't get so mad when the kid in the seat behind you bugs you or that you didn't feel so left out when your friend doesn't ask you to play? Do you wish you weren't afraid when it's your turn to speak in class?

Well, you can change your feelings, just like you are changing a channel on TV! You can use this next breathing game to help you feel more relaxed and to see yourself feeling more positive and in control. Don't try to push your old feelings away. Just focus on new, positive feelings as you breathe.

Place your feet flat on the floor and when you feel comfy, close your eyes. Take three long, deep breaths while you silently count to three: one … two … three. Let your breath out and again count to three: one … two … three.

On the in-breath, say something like this to yourself: "Breathe in sunshine.…" As you let go of the breath, say, "Breathe out clouds."

We bet you already get how this works. On the in-breath, think of something happy and positive that you are breathing in. On the out-breath, think of something negative or stressful that you are letting go of. Got it? Breathe in the positive, breathe out the negative.

Here are some more examples you might want to use:

- Breathe in friendship.… Breathe out loneliness.

- Breathe in relaxation.… Breathe out stress.

- Breathe in happiness.… Breathe out sadness.

- Breathe in bravery.… Breathe out fear.

Activity 18   Breathing Happy Thoughts

In these spaces that follow, write down some positive feelings or things you can breathe in and some negative feelings or things you can breathe out. Then practice changing your feelings with each calming breath.

Breathe in _____. Breathe out _____.

Breathe in _____. Breathe out _____.

Breathe in _____. Breathe out _____.

Breathe in _____. Breathe out _____.

Breathe in _____. Breathe out _____.

The Relaxation & Stress Reduction Workbook for Kids

Chapter 4
Relaxing Through Guided Imagery

Think of a star baseball player up at bat. It's the final game of the World Series. He stands, totally focused on the ball. He pictures its arc coming toward him; he feels his arm muscles unwinding their most powerful swing; he imagines the resounding crack of the bat. He pictures the perfect hit. And then he does it. The crowd roars.

For years, athletes have used powerful mental exercises to enhance their performances. We call these exercises *visualizations* because, in their mind's eye, people see themselves doing exactly what they want to do.

Guided imagery is a form of visualization: a gentle directive meditation that powerfully focuses the imagination. You engage your senses while listening to carefully crafted scripts, either on tape or in person. Research has shown that imagery can have a positive impact on health. Just ten minutes of imagery can fight stress by lowering blood pressure and reducing blood levels of glucose and cholesterol. Guided imagery is used to help people lose weight, reduce anxiety, and lessen aches and pains, as well as to enhance creativity and performance.

Sounds good, doesn't it? Here's how it works. Guided imagery is based on the mind-body connection. Those marvelous brains of ours don't distinguish between imaginary experiences and actual experiences. They send the same cues to our bodies regardless. For example, when we read a wonderful recipe, we start to salivate. The mind is constructing images: how the food looks, smells, tastes, and feels in our mouths. The brain signals the body, and the body says, "Yum! Let's eat!" Then we become hungry.

What you probably don't realize is that you are imagining all the time, since imagery is thought combined with senses. For example, you think of a conflict with your boss. You see her face and you hear the words you said, or wish you'd said, inside your mind. These images now provoke feelings of anger or fear. Your body then responds, except the response is stress, not hunger. For better or worse, the body listens to the mind.

Guided Imagery and Children

Can guided imagery help your child? Think for a moment about how she uses play and fantasy to process the world around her, engaging her imagination. This is why imagery works so well and easily to help children self-heal, problem solve, and relax; it is a natural fit for them.

This technique works by pairing relaxation with imagery. In this state of relaxed focus, people are capable of more rapid healing, growth, and learning. As a guide, you don't "do" anything for your child. She does it herself, which gives her a sense of confidence, accomplishment, and control. By stimulating self-awareness, guided imagery reveals to your child the undiscovered treasures of her inner resources: a true gift.

Getting Started: Some Practical Tips

Guided imagery is a three-step process:

1. Begin with whole body relaxation by doing Activity 19 with your child before every imagery. Remember, relaxation is the launchpad of the experience.

    Note: We suggest you practice the whole body relaxation exercise once or twice to get familiar with how it feels. You could tape it for both of you to use.

2. Guide the experience using the scripts. As you become comfortable, feel free to change a script to fit the needs and preferences of your child. Toward the end of a script, you can ask your child to think of a signal (which can be paired with a touch) you can remind her of later to help her access the positive feelings of the imagery. When ending an imagery, help your child reorient slowly. A glass of water helps as does a hug or a rub on the back. Remember, she has been on a marvelous journey and, like Dorothy at the end of *The Wizard of Oz*, she needs a welcoming transition back home.

3. Do a closure or wrap-up after finishing. This is a time to explore and express what your child has learned and any conflicts she may have had, and also to check in on what parts of the method work better for her. Remember to stay out of the way; you are helping your child find her own answers. Encourage her to draw or write in a journal, or you can jot down a note to help you remember important details.

If your child is working on a particular problem (for example, going to sleep or anxiety before school), plan to practice imagery for fifteen to thirty minutes daily for several weeks. Imagery also works very well in groups.

Introduce your child to the idea of imagery before actually using the technique. We like to call these activities "imagery games" because children are generally more interested in games than exercises! Keep it simple: you are just trying to show her that she can create imagery. Have her practice by closing her eyes, doing a few belly breaths, and creating imagery with different senses. For example:

*   The smell of cookies baking, of pine trees, of flowers, of newly mowed grass

*   The taste of a lemon, of her favorite food (name it)

*   The sound of her father's voice saying her name, of a cat meowing, of the wind blowing through trees

*   The feel of a cat's fur, of sand under her bare feet, of sunshine on her face

Explain that sensing or feeling with the emotions is also a very important way of creating imagery.

A quiet environment where you won't be disturbed is best. Well-chosen soft music will enhance the effects of imagery. Music also becomes a conditioning cue, so if you play the same piece every time, it will become a trigger for her body to relax.

Having your child position her hands the same way every time (for example, two inches below her belly button or over her heart) is another cue; with practice she can take this position anytime and her body will respond as it did in the imagery.

Imagery can bring up many emotions and body sensations. This is natural and normal. As a guide, your most important job is to listen quietly, not to give advice, judge, or interpret. When needed, you can give prompts like "Go on," "Tell me more," or simply "Mmm."

There is no one right way to use this technique. Your skill will increase the more you practice. Also remember that creating imagery is an ongoing and interactive process. Work with your child to make it her own process, adjusting for individual preferences as you go along. Your bond with your child is part of the healing magic. Trust yourself.

Whole Body Relaxation

Activity 19

Do a version of this exercise before every guided imagery activity. First, create a quiet environment and take a few long, deep, focused breaths yourself. Have your child lie on his back with his eyes closed or sit with his feet flat on the floor, hands resting on his thighs just below his belly. If your child does not want to close his eyes, he can choose something in the room to be a focal point. Try to keep the mood open and relaxed. Read the script in a slow, even voice, pausing often.

Whole Body Relaxation Script

You are closing your eyes and beginning to relax. Take some long, slow breaths from deep in your belly. Your belly is getting bigger as you breathe in and smaller as you breathe out. You are not in a hurry, so let yourself be right here, right now. That's good. You are beginning to relax, letting go of anything that is troubling you, letting yourself get quiet. Your whole body relaxes and lets go with each breath. Let go of any pain, breathing in peacefulness and relaxation, breathing out sadness, worry, and stress. That's right. Just let it happen, breathing deeply, relaxing easily. Now let yourself imagine a warm, glowing ball of light above your head. Imagine this warm, relaxing light entering at the top of your head. This light melts over your whole scalp, softening and releasing any places that are tight. Focus on this warm light as it melts over your forehead and face, softening them, melting away tightness, relaxing your eyes, your jaw, your mouth. See the beautiful, healing light move down to your throat and neck area. You can place your hand there. That's right; just let go of the sadness or stress that can live there. It wants to leave. Just let it go—that's good—and some more ... and a little more. Let the warm, glowing light move down the back of your neck into your shoulders, softening your bones, opening and releasing your shoulders. The light swirls down your arms, bringing relaxation to each elbow. Your hands feel warm and heavy. The healing light pushes any stress out through your fingertips. Go to the top of your back and let the light move down each bone in your back, melting and softening, releasing. Let the beautiful light move to the front of your body, and take a deep, letting-go breath. That's good. Breathe the warm light deep into your chest. Put your hand on your heart and let the light wrap around you, letting go of any worry, any sad or mad feelings, any stress. It wants to leave you. Just watch it go ... and some more ... and the last drops. That's right. Take another deep breath and pull the healing light into your belly area, letting it soften and relax. Now let the light flow down each side of your body, moving down into each hip, softening and opening each joint. The whole upper half of your body is completely relaxed. Let the warm light travel into your bottom, relaxing, then flowing down into each leg, releasing stress, warming each knee, then each ankle. The light flows into each foot and into each toe and pushes all the old, stale energy out through a little door in the bottom of your feet. Just let it go. That's good. You have a glowing stream of light flowing in from the top of your head to the bottoms of your feet. It runs healing light through your entire body. Check in with your body and see if there are tight places left over. If so, just breathe into that place, letting it relax. Breathe the light to that part of your body. Take your time. You feel warm and relaxed and safe, like you are floating, filled with relaxation.

This is a wonderful, healing exercise that both children and adults really enjoy. It is the most important of all the imagery exercises because even if your child can't change the circumstances of the external world, he can still access a sense of safety and healing from within.

It is easy to do. Your child will simply use his senses to evoke a wonderful, peaceful place. It can be a real place or one he creates; it doesn't matter. What matters is that it is a personal place of beauty and healing, a safe place where he can go anytime and leave behind pain, frustration, and anger.

This exercise is a little different from the others because your child will give you feedback while you are guiding him. Explain that in this imagery game you want him to answer your questions out loud when you ask them. Be patient while you wait for his responses.

After the imagery, be sure to let your child tell you what it was like there. Did he discover anything new, any surprises? Does he feel different from when you started? Is there a special word or a signal, a sort of magic button that would help him go back there later if he wanted? For example, is there a little toy or object he could touch as a cue?

Remember to do a whole body relaxation before starting the imagery and to read slowly in an even voice, pausing often.

A Special Place Script

Closing your eyes, take long, deep, quiet breaths. Feel your body relax, letting go of any tension. Just feel your breath go in and out. Listen to your breath, saying to yourself, "I am peaceful and relaxed." That's good. Allow an image or picture to form in your mind of a beautiful, peaceful place, a place that feels very healing and safe. Just allow it to come to you. Don't worry if it takes a while. It can be somewhere you've been or maybe a place you've never been. It feels completely safe and is completely yours. Nothing can come in that you don't allow in. When you are there, just nod or raise a finger to let me know. (When your child nods or raises a finger, continue. Keep the pace slow as your child experiences the image.) *That's good. Just notice every detail of what it is like there. Good. What are you seeing? What do you hear?* (Allow your child plenty of time to respond; don't rush this inner work.) *Do you notice any smells? Who is there? Just tell me what comes to you.* (Continue to allow time for responses.) *Good. Now just take a moment to enjoy your safe, special place. Feel how good it feels to be there. What is it like? Okay, great, allow yourself to be like a feeling-sponge, just taking in all the beauty and quiet and safety and healing of your special place. Take it in. It's all yours, so just enjoy it. You can return here anytime you want. Do you know how to do this? Think of a special signal or touch that would remind you of being here and would be a magic button to help you come back. Do you have something? That's good.* (It's okay if your child has not chosen a signal.) *You have the power to come back anytime. When you are ready, begin to return to this room. Take your time. Notice your breathing, in and out. Notice how heavy your arms and legs feel. Begin to notice the sounds in the room. Slowly begin to open your eyes. You're feeling relaxed and comfortable. You feel all nice and new from your visit to your special place.*

The Relaxation & Stress Reduction Workbook for Kids

Most children respond enthusiastically to the idea of an imaginary helper who can give them power and guidance in facing challenges. Fairy tales are full of such characters. The helper might be an animal with qualities your child needs: a wise owl to help with a reading test, a playful dolphin to help a shy child join the fun on the playground, or a brave lion to help boost courage before a doctor's visit. The helper might be a guardian angel, a spiritual figure, or even a family member. What's important is that your child meets her inner helper in the process of the exercise and that the inner helper represents wisdom, support, love, and safety to the child. She can use the "gifts" or "advice" from the inner helper to solve problems or simply to receive comfort in a stressful situation. Naturally, you will want to present the idea in a way that is consistent with your values and beliefs. Just remember your role is to listen, be patient, and give your child time to do the work.

Allow time afterward for your child to tell you all about her inner helper or helpers, because a child can have more than one. What did it feel like to meet? What did she discover? What was surprising? Was the image helpful? Does she feel different than she did before the exercise? You could also have your child draw a picture of herself meeting the helper, and hang it up in a visible place.

Once a child begins to trust imagery, it can grow and help in many different ways. Prepare to be surprised.

Be sure to do a whole body relaxation exercise before this exercise. Remember to use a slow, even voice, and pause frequently.

Inner Helpers Script

You are focusing on your belly breathing: deep, quiet breaths, just letting your whole body relax, letting any tension just drain out through your toes. That's good. Listening to your breath, you are feeling comfortable and relaxed. Now that you are quiet, go to your special place and let yourself feel how good it is there. That's right. Take your time. Now let a picture or image come to you. It may be just a feeling. It is very kind and nice. It is there to help you. It wants only good things for you. It can be anything: an animal … a person … an angel. Just let it come and get clearer. (Give your child time and encouragement while the image forms.) Your helper inside you is very wise and loves you very much. It is here to help you with any problem or any question you have. Just let it come. Take your time until your helper shows up. When you are ready, give a nod. Take a minute to get comfortable now that your helper is here. What does it look like? Tell me about it. (Allow your child time to answer.) That's good. Ask your helper if it has a name. Take your time. Just let it talk to you and answer it back. There is no hurry. Ask for help with a problem you are having: what you need to know, what you need to do so that the problem can get smaller or so that you don't have to feel so bad. It is there to help you. It may bring you a feeling, a thought, anything. Whatever it brings, this is the gift to you. What is it bringing you? (Allow your child time to answer.) Good. Whatever it brings you will help you with your problem; it will help you to feel brave and safe.

Ask your helper any other questions about the gift. Take your time. When you are finished, say "Thank you" to your helper for coming. You may want to give it a gift yourself to say "Thank you." Take all the time you need. That's good. When you feel ready, focus on your belly breathing again. Slowly begin to return to the room. Start to hear the sounds and slowly begin to open your eyes. You are feeling wonderful and relaxed and so lucky to have a special friend to help you whenever you need it.

The Healing Rainbow

This imagery can be used to reduce pain. Have your child lie down or sit comfortably with both feet on the floor, hands resting on his legs with his palms up, eyes closed. Be sure to do a whole body relaxation exercise first, and then follow the four steps below before reading the script on the next page:

1. Ask your child where in his body he is feeling pain.

2. Have him tell you how much pain he is feeling, using a scale from 1 to 10, with 10 being the highest. Young children sometimes do better showing you with their outstretched hands how small or big their discomfort is. You can show a young child that hands together means no pain at all. During and after the imagery, you will ask your child to tell you again how big his pain is. Usually it will have decreased or disappeared.

3. Ask what it looks like, what color it is. What shape is it? Simply accept what he says and give positive responses. Ask what it looks like. Is it warm or cold? There are no right answers. In this imagery the child is interacting with the image and describing to you what is happening.

4. Ask what color his "healing power" should be. Pain can make us feel helpless. Choosing a magic color for healing can help restore a sense of choice and control. Tell your child that the images inside our minds change and the color or feel of the pain or even the healing color might shift as he uses his relaxation and imagination powers to work with it. This is perfectly fine. Again, the goal is to openly and respectfully receive whatever comes up for your child. Be patient with the process.

The Healing Rainbow Script

Now you are taking deep breaths in and out, quieting your body, just following the feeling of your breath. That's right. You are letting any tightness in your body just loosen and soften around the pain. Let yourself imagine a bright, healing rainbow with every magic color you need. It is just waiting to flow in and help you. It can flow in through the top of your head or up through the bottom of your feet or anywhere you want it to. Allow it to flow into you. That's good. Now let your healing color flow over any feelings of the (child's description of the pain here) *pain or tension. They are just feelings and they want to leave you, so let them leave. That's right; let a little more leave … and even some more. That's good. Just keep letting your breath be long and slow. Deep belly breathing. That's right. Now I am going to ask you to check in with yourself. Letting your eyes stay closed, what color is the pain now? Go ahead; tell me.* (Listen for your child's response.) *Okay, what shape is it? How big is it?* (Allow plenty of time for your child's responses. The color, shape, or image of the pain has likely changed; this is fine.) *Can you give me a number from 1 to 10 that shows how big it is? Just let it come to you. Good. Let yourself take deep, quiet breaths again, breathing from your belly, staying calm and relaxed. See and feel your healing rainbow. Let your magic healing color flow over any pain that is still there. Staying relaxed, just let it happen allowing the* (color, shape, or image of the pain your child had described) *pain to get smaller. Remember, it's just a feeling and it wants to leave with your powerful healing color. You can let it go. That's right … and some more … and even some more. Now check in with yourself. What color is the pain now? How big is it? And what is your pain number now? Good. Now you are going back to your belly breathing, feeling relaxed, allowing yourself to see and feel your rainbow and your magic healing color. That's right. Use your healing color to work with it some more. You can do it. Remember, it is just a feeling. It wants to leave; can you let it go? That's good … and some more … and even some more. You are feeling better now. Your body is more comfortable, and your pain is less. Maybe it has even gone. Let yourself bring this healing feeling back with you today. As much of it as you need, you have the power to bring. When you are ready, begin to come back to the room, taking your time, thinking of your breathing again, noticing the sounds of the room. Slowly, gently begin opening your eyes. Your body feels relaxed and comfortable. It feels good to know you can help yourself whenever you need to.*

Do a whole body relaxation exercise with your child first. Very soft background music without lyrics can help create a nighttime relaxation ritual. Guided imagery works best when it feels comfortable to you and your child, so feel free to be creative with the details of the imagery, incorporating favorite colors, animals, special likes, or spiritual beliefs. Remember to read slowly in an even voice, with frequent pauses to allow time for the imagery to form in your child's imagination.

Island of the Sleeping Ponies Script

As you let yourself become comfortable and relaxed, imagine it is a warm summer evening. The sun is low in the sky, and its golden rays shine softly on you as you stand on the edge of a beautiful, sparkling bay. Off in the distance you spy a little island with a grassy meadow on it. You would love to go but you have no way to get there. As you stand here, let yourself see, hear, smell, and feel everything around you. You feel so peaceful as the wind softly strokes your cheeks and your face and your hair. There are birds swooping and darting against the deep blue sky, calling out to each other. You hear a splash as a fish jumps in the water. The waves are lapping against the shore. You feel happy to be here with your toes in the water. You did not even notice at first that a little blue boat is coming toward you; what could this be? Quietly the little boat glides to a stop in front of you. Deep and sturdy, it has several snug, red, cushiony seats built into it. You sense that this is a safe, magic boat and at that very moment you spy a piece of paper. It has your name on it: (Say your child's name). Unfolding the paper, you read a message meant especially for you. It says, "You are relaxed and safe. Please get in and come." And you do.

The little boat begins to journey out from the land. The boat is carrying you toward the island with the grassy meadow. It moves smoothly, like a dolphin gliding through the water. You are feeling safe in the sturdy little boat as the deep, slanting rays of golden sun light up everything around you. You are filled with wonder. You love the smell of the fresh salt air. Everything seems to shine with a magic gold and blue light.

As you approach the shore, you hear a high barking sound. Looking out over the side of your boat into the water, you see a shiny little seal with gray eyes, watching you. His whiskers are long, and his small face is so kind and gentle. He is a shy creature, and in his mouth he is carrying something for you, hanging in a little bag. Slowly, carefully you reach over the side and pat his sleek little head, ever so softly. His eyes close. Then with his nose he nudges you and the bag slides onto your hand. He dips his head and is gone. Good-bye. You look in the little bag, and it is filled with apples and carrots.

As the boat lands, you step out onto the soft sand. The grass is very tall around the beach, but a white gull lands to show you the way to a hidden path. The path curves around, and suddenly you are in the most beautiful meadow. The scent of blossoms, sweet grasses, and pines from the forest behind rises to your nose, and you breathe in deeply, almost drinking the wonderful smell. Suddenly you are aware of eyes watching you. The meadow is filled with small golden-haired ponies standing completely still, watching you. Their manes and tails are so full and fluffy. You slowly walk up to one of them and you are smiling. Instead of running away, it nuzzles your hand, as though it has been waiting for you to come.

It is the most magic moment and you are so happy. Pretty soon, the other little ponies come toward you. They are not afraid; they all seem to want to be your friends. They make soft, whinnying sounds and when they look at you, they have the biggest eyes, like dark, melted chocolate. They lean against you with total trust.

Then you remember the seal's gift, and you take out an apple and a carrot for each pony. They eat them from your hands, their tongues rough but gentle. They lick your hands clean, and one even nuzzles its face right up to yours. You feel so special and so calm. Then you hear a slight snorting, and the mother horse comes out of the woods into the meadow. All the ponies amble over to her, and she leans down with her long neck and nuzzles each one. Many just want to lean against her, and they do.

Now the sun has dipped beneath the land, and you see the first lone star come out, even as the last streaks of rose and orange fade away. It is time for sleep. The mother walks around all the ponies, herding them together. One by one, they lie down in the sweet grass, their heads resting on each other's bellies, their eyes closing in sleep. She walks over to you, too, and gazes at you with love and caring in her liquid brown eyes. You are feeling very safe and relaxed and very sleepy, so you, too, lie down, your face against the warm hide of a sleeping friend beside you. You feel yourself drifting off to sleep. The mother will take care of you; you know this. You are a special part of this circle on the island of the sleeping ponies.

Strengthening Self-Esteem

This exercise requires only five to ten minutes. In this script there are pauses as your child actively interacts with her image. Tell your child you will be doing an imagery game that involves her favorite animal, storybook figure, or hero. Be sure to do a whole body relaxation before starting the imagery and save time at the end to wrap up the exercise by listening to your child's experience.

Remember When Script

You are taking quiet, deep breaths, just allowing your body and mind to feel relaxed and like liquid. You are letting go of any tightness anywhere in your body. That's right. Breathing deeply, listening to your breath go in and out. That's good.

Let yourself see in your mind a picture of your favorite animal (or storybook figure or hero). Just give me the signal when you can picture or feel this animal really strongly. (Wait for your child's signal.) See what you love and admire about this animal. Let the feeling get stronger; let yourself have any feelings about the wonderful qualities of your animal. That's good. Now let yourself see a time when you were like your animal in any way, a time when you yourself showed some of the same qualities. Take your time, let it come. If this is hard, ask your animal for help. Remember where you were and what you were doing when you had some of these qualities; notice how you felt. Take this feeling now and let it get bigger ... and even bigger. Imagine you are turning up the volume button on this good feeling. Take this feeling and allow it help you in any way you need. It's yours. Imagine using it for a problem you are having now. How does it feel? Do you think it can help? Just stay with it for a little bit. That's right. This feeling is yours. Anytime you want it, you can just use your relaxing breath and call up the picture of your animal in your mind, and this feeling can come back to you. When you are ready, let yourself slowly begin to come back to the room. Listen to your breathing. Hear the sounds slowly. Slowly open your eyes just a little bit. You are peaceful and relaxed, and you can use your animal image and the strength it gives you anyplace, anytime.

Activity 25

Floating Away from Stress

This imagery exercise is more like a story. As in Activity 23, your child does not share out loud during the process. You could also try this with a group of children; imagery works wells in groups. Be creative: at a sleepover, you might introduce it as a relaxation game to help kids settle down. Have them become quiet and do a brief whole body relaxation first. Remember to keep your voice even and to read slowly.

The Balloon Ride Script

Did you ever see someone just let go of a balloon on a string? Did you watch it float up? It's hard to take your eyes off that.

What if we could let go of our worries, problems, and mixed-up feelings, and allow them to just float away out of sight? That would feel good. Or we could take a trip up in a balloon ourselves, the kind you can ride in. We are going to relax our bodies and our minds and see where the wind takes us. Ready? Good.

First, just let yourself get comfy wherever you are lying or sitting. If you are sitting, uncross your legs and put your feet on the ground. Let your head hang down and let your hands rest on your thighs. If you are lying down, rest your hands a little below your belly button so you can feel your own balloon breathe in and out as you relax. Let your eyes close. Notice your breathing and let it become very easy. Feel all your muscles relax and let go. That's good. Feel your heartbeat slow down and say to yourself, "I am relaxed." Take three long, deep breaths, and let your out-breath be a let-it-all-go breath. Notice how good that feels. Notice where there is any tightness in your body, and let each breath carry it away. That's right.

Imagine now that you are in a big field, and in the middle of the field is an enormous hot-air balloon. The balloon has so many different beautiful colors and a comfy basket for you to ride in. The basket is safely tied to the balloon, which is controlled magically by hot air inside it. Just stay relaxed, and notice what is going on. There is no right or wrong way to imagine this. What colors do you see in your balloon? Can you hear the whooshing sound of air that fills it up and makes it want to rise? It makes a wonderful sound, long and slow. There are ropes holding it to the earth. Can you touch them and feel what they feel like?

You are feeling completely safe and completely relaxed on this trip, and maybe you will want to go with a special friend or a grown-up who feels really safe. Or maybe you'll just want to go by yourself. Or with your dog or cat or favorite stuffed animal; however you feel safe and relaxed is good.

As you get into the basket, you can hear the great whooshing sound of the balloon's air, almost like deep, slow breaths in and out. The big ropes are released and you are lifted off, going up, up, up. And you're feeling completely safe and completely relaxed.

The field, the big trees on the ground, the houses, everything below you seems to be growing smaller as you float higher and higher. Can you see anything else below you? Birds? Clouds? Boats on a lake?

Just notice them. Say to yourself again, "I am relaxed." It feels so good to just float away. The sky is like a big, blue dream, and you can feel the gentle wind blow across your face. You can feel the warmth of the sun on your skin. It feels good. You can hear the creaking of the ropes and the quiet whoosh of the balloon. As you continue to rise, you feel every muscle become loose and relaxed. Anything that you were worrying about before you left, any big feeling you had, any problems are just getting smaller and smaller, and it feels so good to let them go, and you say again to yourself, "I am relaxed."

As you look out over the edge of the basket, you see that you are floating over the tops of the highest mountains. You are passing over the tallest buildings in the biggest cities, over the jungle, and over the ocean. There is only wind and air and light and a happy feeling of being safe and free. Notice how this feels in your body. Just enjoy how good it feels.

Now slowly, slowly the balloon begins to gently descend, to get lower. You begin to see shapes on the ground, the tops of trees, and the roofs of houses with their chimneys. Cars on the streets look tiny but are slowly getting bigger. Remember as you come back you are bringing with you that magical, peaceful feeling of relaxation and calm. You see the field beneath you as you gently, gently move nearer, downward toward it.

Finally you are almost on the ground. With a gentle thud, the balloon basket touches, and when you are ready, you step out. Take your time. You feel the bottom of your feet touching the earth. It's been a wonderful ride. You say to yourself, "I feel calm and relaxed." Slowly, when you are ready, open your eyes. Just stretch a little now. Notice how good you feel when your body and mind are relaxed. Remember that anytime you feel worried or feel like problems are too big, you have the power to relax and make them get little. Remember this special balloon ride and what you saw and how good it felt. And you can return here and go up anytime, using your breath. It's all yours.

As you read this imagery aloud, remember to use a slow, even voice. Read it as you would a fairy tale, but softly. At the end, let your voice slow down and allow your child to remain quiet and inwardly focused. Remind him that he can bring back this pain-free or pain-reduced feeling and take it with him into his day. Ask what the experience was like and let your child tell you what worked for him. He might want to draw a picture of it.

There is no one right way to do it. If your child saw electric-pink dolphins instead of blue ones, that is wonderful: he is accessing his own unique inner healing power!

The Rescue Dolphins Script

Your tummy doesn't feel good at all. It feels achy or like it could turn itself right upside down, or both! (Substitute whatever symptom your child is complaining about; for example, pain or nausea.) *You want to feel better, but those little gray, nasty fish are swimming around in your stomach, making it hurt and feel yucky. Making slimy black knots in the tummies of little kids is what they love to do. But you have the power to fight them. Yes, you do. Just relax and believe.*

Close your eyes gently and take three slow, deep breaths. That's right. Say to yourself, "I am relaxed." Imagine you hear the gurgle and rush of a stream of crystal-clear water. Where is it coming from? you wonder. You see a sparkling, turquoise-blue river flowing toward you from the sea, and swimming in the river are one hundred blue dolphins, jumping and diving and making little squeaking dolphin noises. They heard your call and are on their way to help you. They can come in through a little door in your belly button, and that is exactly what they do. It feels good, because the blue dolphins are not only very playful, they are also very powerful and hungry, and the nasty knot-fish don't like to see them coming. As the dolphins fill your belly, you feel immediately better. You feel their love and their strength.

As they swim up to the nasty knot-fish, they jump and dive all around them. The knot-fish try to find somewhere to swim, but the blue rescue dolphins are too quick. They are smiling and laughing as they eat up every single knot-fish and untie all the knots. The blue dolphins are so clever that the dark knots that were so tight just dissolve and melt right away. The blue dolphins have worked their magic; the water around them is now cleansing and your tummy is feeling much better. You feel healthy and happy to have such wonderful friends who love you and will come to your rescue anytime you call them.

Chapter 5
Mindfulness: A New Way to Deal with Stress

The practice of mindful meditation has been around for thousands of years, yet this Buddhist concept is not related just to meditation or spiritual practice. In the last decade, mindfulness has been used to treat a variety of psychological problems, and it is now thought to be an important preventive activity, helping to reduce the myriad stresses of daily life.

Dr. Jon Kabat-Zinn, founder of the stress reduction program at the University of Massachusetts Medical School, has been the pioneer of the mindfulness movement in stress reduction. In *Wherever You Go, There You Are: Mindfulness Meditation in Everyday Life* (1994, Hyperion), he writes:

> Mindfulness means paying attention in a particular way: on purpose, in the present moment, and nonjudgmentally. This kind of attention nurtures greater awareness, clarity, and acceptance of present moment reality. It wakes us to the fact that our lives unfold only in moments. If we are not present for those moments, we may not only miss what is valuable in our lives but also fail to realize the richness and depth of our possibilities for growth and transformation (p. 4).

The practice of mindfulness involves focusing your attention fully on whatever you are experiencing from moment to moment. Ordinarily, attention is like a light with a broad beam: it lights up a pretty big area, but not too brightly. Mindfulness is like a very powerful light shining intensely on one small point. It is a tool to help you and your child learn to focus your attention in the present moment and by doing so, release your mind's tight grip on worrying about the future or thinking about the past.

To give you a taste of how it works, close your eyes and take a couple of minutes to be mindful of all the sounds around you. Don't strain to hear them or figure them out; just take them in as pure sound. Listen for silence, the space between the sounds, as well. If you hear a dog bark and start thinking about your dog or how annoying it is to pick up the neighbor's dog's poop from your yard, your mind is wandering. This is very normal. Gently guide it back. If you hear a jackhammer on the street and think, "What a horrible noise!" just gently notice your reaction and bring your attention back. Do you feel different after this experience? How?

Here is another brief exercise that shows how mindfulness can shift your experience. Focus on an object in nature: perhaps a stone, a leaf, a tree, a cloud, or a flower. Close your eyes first and focus on your breathing, using the belly breathing we described earlier. Then open them and become totally present to your object with your senses—sight, smell, sound, touch.

Try this for five minutes. You will have thoughts; that's normal. Just observe them and let them go. What do you notice?

As family members, most of us are just too busy with competing demands. We are catapulted into our days like rockets off a launchpad: this is not a fun feeling, no matter how many things get checked off the to-do list. Mindfulness practice is the opposite of trying to get something done. As Kabat-Zinn says, "The best way to get somewhere is to let go of trying to get anywhere at all" (p. 16).

Remember that your children will follow the behaviors you consistently model in your own life for dealing with stress, so just like other tools in this book, the practice of mindfulness helps parents first, then children. Think about it: how many calm, happy children of highly stressed parents have you known?

Note to Parents

If you are like most parents, you have to tell your children to slow down while they eat and to actually chew their food. This is not just parental harping. There are real medical reasons for not allowing your kids to eat the way your dog eats! Chewing starts the process of digestion and ultimately aids in increased absorption of vitamins and nutrients in the small intestines. Additionally, our stomachs require about twenty minutes to signal our brains that we are full so that we do not overeat. The National Centers for Disease Control and Prevention has named childhood obesity as a national epidemic: there are more overweight children in this country than ever before. Of course, this certainly may not apply to you, but we have observed that many grown-ups eat too fast as well.

Mealtime is a primary bonding time for many families, sometimes the only time family members are all together. We have worked with families who had many sources of stress and sometimes very few economic resources, but the ones who had the most closeness seemed to have at least one thing in common: they ate together as a family on a regular basis.

So take a moment to reflect. What are mealtimes like for your family? How could they be more relaxing? We hope you'll give mindful eating a try.

If you are like most kids, someone has probably told you a bunch of times to keep your mouth closed when you eat or to slow down or maybe to keep your hands out of your noodles. You wouldn't eat with your hands anyway, right? A lot of kids (and grown-ups, too) eat while they are doing other things, like riding in the car, watching TV, or even cruising down the street on a skateboard.

There are good reasons to slow down and pay attention to what you are eating. It is much healthier, for one. But what's important here is this: learning to pay attention to what you're eating can help you stay calm and focused. That can help your day go better and make you feel really, really good. When you are having a horrible, no-good day, chances are you are stressed and feel like pieces of you are everywhere.

Mindful eating is one more tool in your relaxation toolbox. It means paying attention to what you are eating with all your senses: touching, seeing, hearing, smelling, and, of course, tasting. It can be fun. You can ask your mom or dad or maybe even your brother or sister to try it with you. If you do that, the only rule is silence.

Ask Mom or Dad if you can practice with a food you really like. Get it and sit at the table with it in front of you. Before you begin, take a few deep belly breaths, the real letting-go type of breaths that you have been practicing. Then, start to eat with your eyes. That's right! Your first job is to really look at your food and experience it through your eyes. Here's a challenge: for one minute, just look at what you are about to eat and notice everything about it. Can you do this for a whole minute without thinking about the time, just about how the food looks?

Here's what a kid named David noticed when he tried eating with his eyes: "Right now, I am looking at one small square of very dark chocolate. It's actually not a square, it's a rectangle. It looks like a tiny dark-brown brick. There is a little place in the corner where it's scratched so that place is lighter. The top edge is rounded."

Did you do a whole minute of just paying attention with your eyes? Really?

Next, use your nose. Go ahead and really smell what you are about to eat. Smelling is wonderful, but we hardly ever pay attention with our noses! Try closing your eyes to help you focus on one sensation at a time. David said, "My chocolate smells kind of deep and dark and sweet, like my dad's coffee." What does your food smell like?

If you haven't already done it, go ahead and touch your food. Make sure you have a napkin nearby. Close your eyes. What does it feel like? Is it soft or hard or rubbery? Okay, great! Now clean your hand.

Now we are going to ask you to do something your teacher never will: use your mouth to pay attention! That's right. V-e-r-y s-l-o-w-l-y taste your food. Don't chew it yet; just let it sit on your tongue for a while. The challenge is to concentrate only on the taste. Go slowly.

You can start to chew now. David's chocolate didn't make any noise at all. Does your food make any noise when you chew it? What about the feeling in your mouth? Is it smooth or crunchy or slippery like Jell-O? Do you notice anything about your food that you never noticed before? Is the taste one flavor or many flavors?

Don't focus on whether you like what you are eating; just experience it. If your attention starts to wander all around like a puppy off a leash, you have stopped noticing with your mouth. If you find yourself thinking about a new video game or that annoying kid who sits behind you at school, just gently bring yourself back to tasting, moment by moment, as you finish your food. When you practice mindfulness, think only about the present moment, not about this morning or tonight. Use all your senses to focus. This is where the powerful magic is. This is what helps you calm yourself.

Activity 28　Mindfulness with a Pet

Note to Parents

Read over this activity with your child, and choose a time when he will practice it. Some words of wisdom about children and dogs: Children should always be supervised around animals that are not family pets. In the world of dog communication, it is very threatening to look directly into a dog's eyes. Also, many dogs do not like being hugged by children. Teach your child ahead of time how to approach the animal respectfully, which means slowly and gently and without direct eye contact. You want him to know this anyway, particularly with strange dogs, to avoid being bitten. (Good manners with other people's pets is also just a good thing in general!)

If your pet is a dog, lucky you. Just make sure you know whether your dog has been socialized to accept hugging or other interactions that involve being near to its face. We are not trying to teach fear, but rather respect based on learning through careful observation and interaction. And wouldn't it be great if we approached people more often like this?

Be sure to give your child just a couple of minutes afterward to tell you what new things he noticed and how he feels: more relaxed or less relaxed. Accept with interest whatever your child tells you. Children love to talk about their pets, and you may be amazed by his powers of observation!

Here is another stress-busting idea: try the activity yourself. Or try it together for five minutes without speaking. In a noisy, intrusive world, practicing silence is a calming act.

If you have a pet of any kind, whether it is a dog or a cat or a hamster or even a fish, this is a great activity to help you relax and really get to know your pet even more than you already do.

Pets are not only fun, they can also help us feel calmer, more focused, and more loving. Whenever we feel interest and love for something, we let go of whatever other nasty feelings are bothering us. Your brain is made to hold and pay attention to only one thought at a time. But here's a really cool thing: you have the power to change the channel in your brain! If you don't like the program that's playing, change the channel by changing what you are paying attention to.

Find a spot in your home where you can be with your pet without the TV playing or a lot of other stuff going on. First, take three long, deep, relaxing breaths. Deepening and slowing your breathing is always the first step in the magic of mindfulness, so once you have done this, you have invited in the magic. Good for you!

Remember, there is no right or wrong way of being mindful. It isn't like math where there is one right answer. There is only what you notice as you gently pay close attention. The trick in mindfulness is this: staying focused on one thing at a time. Pay attention deeply to that thing only. If your thoughts wander off the path, gently bring them back to this very moment. Star athletes have had to learn to focus this way.

Okay, are you ready? Now really look at your pet, but don't stare directly into its eyes; many animals, especially dogs, don't like this. Notice everything with your eyes. What shape is your pet? Is it rough or smooth or furry or scaly? Notice how big its body is compared to your body. Pay attention with your eyes. Take your time. Does your pet move slowly or quickly? What do you feel like when you do this?

If you can safely or easily pick up or pat your pet, go ahead. Of course, if your pet is a whale or a snapping turtle, this may not be a good idea! Use your good old brain first to make a smart choice, then pay attention through your hands. Move gently and slowly—remember, you probably don't like people sneaking up and touching you.

How does your pet feel? Just notice. What does it do when you touch it? Maybe it doesn't like to be touched, and that's okay. Notice what your pet seems to like. When you start really noticing how your pet reacts to touch, your mindfulness magic is growing stronger.

Use your sense of smell now. What does your pet smell like—an old rug after it has been vacuumed or a barn where warm old cows once lived? Breathe in deeply and make friends with your pet through your sense of smell. Chances are, it is smelling you, too.

Does your pet make any sounds—a cheep, a chirp, a hiss, or a meow? Just notice. Notice every single thing. Keep your attention fully on your animal. Notice how it relaxes. If your pet can't relax when you are touching it, touch it more slowly and gently, or put it down and see what it does. How do you know when your pet feels good or when it is upset?

Try to pay attention with your senses for at least five minutes and then come back to the world of humans. How do you feel? Did you learn anything new about your pet? Do you feel more relaxed now that you've practiced your mindfulness magic? We hope so.

If you do any kind of sport, you may have heard your coach say that your attitude—the way you look at things—affects how you do and how you feel. This is true with everything, even things like doing chores. Chores are little jobs that you just have to do like taking a bath or brushing your teeth, because they are part of everyday living. They are also things that grown-ups ask you to do to help around the house, like sweeping the floor, putting away your toys, emptying the dishwasher, or setting the table.

Do you think that complaining, turning on the TV, or even hiding under your bed when your mom asks you to do something makes it easier or harder to do the chore? Your mind is probably thinking, "I don't want to do this" or "It's too boring" or "It's too hard." These thoughts make jobs even more stressful! Plus, imagine your mom coming in a third time to tell you to please set the table before dinner. Is she more happy or less happy with you? You guessed it—she is less happy. She may even be growling now, changing from a koala into a tiger. Eek—that's too much stress!

So what can you do instead? Practice mindfulness magic with a chore. Remember that mindfulness is simply paying attention by focusing on one thing, whatever you are experiencing, from moment to moment. For example, if you are setting the table, pay attention to the silverware. How heavy or light is it? What does it feel like in your hands? Notice how you arrange it on the table and then notice the plates. What shape are they? What sound do they make as you put them on the table? How do the napkins feel?

What if your thoughts drift to your homework or you start thinking that you don't like the peas you're going to have for dinner or that your little sister is a brat? Just gently bring your whole attention back to what you are doing right now. By paying attention moment to moment, you block out other thoughts. Your mind has become like a hound dog that sniffs and notices everything on the trail. The dog doesn't think, "Oh that smell is good, but this one is really bad!" It just keeps on smelling. So if your thoughts wander, be like that hound dog: keep on the trail of what you are doing.

Below is a list of different chores. Try picking one to practice your mindfulness magic on. The best time to do this is when you or the grown-ups around you are not in a big hurry. Tell your mom or dad about your experiment before you start. Maybe they will want to try practicing, too.

After you are finished, check in with yourself to see how you feel. What did you notice that you never noticed before? Did it feel easier or harder to do your chore? Do you feel more peaceful or more stressed? Remember, when you are learning any magic, it takes time. The more you practice, the stronger you will become; try it and discover for yourself. Choose a chore to practice with:

Brushing your teeth	Putting away clothes
Washing your face	Setting the table
Making your bed	Clearing the table
Sweeping	Picking up your toys
Dusting	Folding clean laundry

Chore I practiced with: _____

Something new or different I noticed: _____

Was it easier or harder to do the chore? _____

How stressed or peaceful I felt afterward (rate yourself on a scale from 1 to 10, with 1 being completely relaxed and 10 being totally stressed): _____.

Did you know that your brain is created to respond positively to nature? That's right. The natural world is like marvelous medicine for your brain—and it doesn't even taste bad. Scientists have found that people who just look at pictures of nature cope better with stress than people who don't. But you may have guessed this anyway, deep down. Think of the last time you spent a day or even an afternoon outside, perhaps at the beach or a park, or maybe just playing in your yard. We bet you felt different when you finally went inside. Maybe you didn't even want to go in.

In this mindfulness magic game, your special mission involves being outside. Be sure to get your mom's or dad's permission because they need to know where you are.

You are going to be in your own yard. If you don't have one, you can go to a park or some nearby outside place, but take Mom or Dad with you. And remember, once you are doing mindfulness magic, you can't talk. Talking breaks the power of your focus.

Okay, first take a few slow, deep, relaxing breaths, then start to walk the outside edge of your yard. With your eyes, just notice everything that is on your path. Do you see anything you've never really noticed before? Walk slowly so that you don't miss anything, and just notice how things look. Pretend you've never seen them before. If you have thoughts about other things, let them pass, and bring your attention back to what you are seeing.

Next, walk around again, this time listening to the world outside your house. Don't strain your ears trying to hear things; let the secret music that is already there come to you. The sounds may be pleasant or not. That's okay. We bet you'll be amazed by all the different sounds you'll notice. If it's really quiet … well, maybe you live at the North Pole—just kidding! If it is quiet, listen for the quiet, the spaces between the sounds. If you want to stop and close your eyes for a bit, that's okay.

Now we bet you can guess.… Yes, you're right. Walk around your yard again, this time using your nose. Remember that hound dog we talked about, the one who just sticks to the scent of things? Be like that dog. We bet you have never ever done this before.

Your noticing powers must be getting pretty good by now, but there's still more. Here is the last bit: Walk the edge of your yard going in the opposite direction. Once again, use your senses of sight, hearing, and smelling. Pretend you are an animal, sensing your way around the yard. Move slowly or you might miss something.

When you are all done, close your eyes and say thank you for all the things you have seen, all the different things you have smelled and heard, whether they pleased you or not. You can also notice that it really is great to be able to see and hear and smell and move. If you cannot do all those things, then you really know how great it is to be able to do some of them. It is wonderful to notice and appreciate things.

Chapter 6
Yoga for Kids

"Arch your back like a cat." "Get up like a dog." "Balance yourself like a boat."

These are the directions that you will give your child to help him learn the ancient practice of yoga. Sounds like fun, doesn't it? No wonder yoga has become one of the most popular ways to teach children how to find calm and peace in body and soul.

The word "yoga" comes from the ancient Sanskrit language, which was spoken by the Brahmins, the religious elite of India. The word is most commonly translated as "union," and yoga is meant to bring together mind, body, and spirit. It has been practiced in many different forms for more than five thousand years. While it was introduced to Americans more than one hundred years ago, it first became part of the mainstream culture in the 1960s, largely due to the interest of four British musicians—John, Paul, George, and Ringo—in Transcendental Meditation, a form of yoga. Today, you will find yoga classes offered in nearly every gym across the country, and it is slowly being introduced to children through yoga centers and even school classrooms.

The positive effects of yoga for children are exactly the same as for adults. It is a form of exercise that promotes strength, coordination, and flexibility. Although any exercise will help reduce stress, yoga also teaches children how to relax and concentrate, combining breathing and mindfulness—and fun! Every child will benefit from its practice, but it can be particularly helpful for children with special needs. It has proved beneficial for children who have physical disabilities, with children who have ADHD or other behavioral disorders, and with children on the autism spectrum.

When you introduce yoga to your child, make sure he is wearing comfortable, loose-fitting clothes. A T-shirt and shorts will do fine. Yoga is practiced with bare feet, so make sure your child does the exercise on a nonslip floor. No special equipment is needed, although children may enjoy having their own yoga mats, which will make some of the poses more comfortable.

This chapter will introduce you and your child to only a small sample of poses. We have divided them into four activities—breathing, stretching, focus and balance, and calming—with two poses in each activity. We recommend that you start with a warm-up period, then do the poses in order, ending with the Dead Man's Pose, which provides a quiet-down. We have been recommending ten- to fifteen-minute relaxation activities for children throughout this book, but the practice of yoga will take a little longer.

Some people have made yoga part of their spiritual life and practice it for several hours every day. But for most children, practicing yoga two or three times a week will be fine. It is important to emphasize to your child that yoga is not a competitive exercise. The poses we will describe in this chapter are simple, but many advanced poses require the strength and balance of a gymnast. Some children will want to test their bodies in the most complicated poses, and they should be discouraged from doing this. Similarly, some children will be inclined to hold their poses for as long as possible, even when they may be uncomfortable. Poses should be held only for a couple of breaths for younger children and a little longer for older children. There is no prize for endurance.

> **CAUTION:** If your child has physical health problems or disabilities, you should consult with your pediatrician or a physical therapist before beginning yoga exercises.

As we mentioned earlier, the key to introducing yoga as a relaxation and stress-reduction technique can be found in one word: "fun." And the key to having fun can be found in another word: "you." If you enjoy doing yoga yourself and bring this enthusiasm to your child, then we are confident that the age-old wisdom of this method will be useful.

Breathing

Correct breathing is important in yoga, just as it is in all of the other forms of relaxation in this book. You may want to practice belly breathing before you begin these poses.

Hold each pose for ten to thirty seconds, depending on the age and interest of the child.

The Mountain

1. Stand with your feet slightly apart and parallel.

2. Feel that you are anchored to the floor.

3. Keep your legs straight and your weight on your heels.

4. Practice belly breathing.

The Cat

1. Kneel on all fours with your palms flat on the floor.

2. As you breathe out, hollow your back, keeping your arms straight.

3. On the next out-breath, arch your back.

4. On the next out-breath, come back to the original position.

Stretching is a great way to loosen your muscles and let all the tension go from your body. You may want to do stretching postures along with breathing exercises before other relaxation activities in this book.

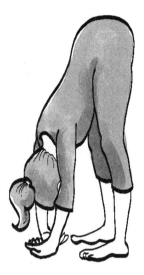

The Rag Doll

1. Stand straight and tall.

2. Bend straight down from the hips, keeping your weight even on both feet.

3. Let your arms hang limply down to the floor.

The Dog

1. Start off on all fours with the palms of your hands on the floor.

2. Breathe out, tuck your toes under, and lift up your hips and buttocks.

3. Slowly straighten your legs.

4. Now stretch, putting your weight on your heels and straightening your arms and legs. Your body should be in the shape of a triangle.

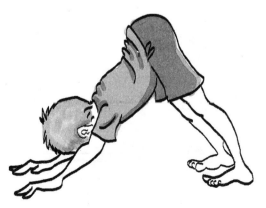

Yoga will help you bring your mind and body together. Did you know that lots of athletes, scientists, artists, and famous performers practice yoga to help them relax, deal with stress, and focus their creative energy?

The Boat

1. Sit tall on a mat with your feet on the ground, hugging your knees.

2. Lean back and put your arms behind your back.

3. Point your toes and lift your legs.

4. Stretch out your arms and balance.

The Airplane

1. Stand straight and tall.

2. Stretch one leg back while you breathe.

3. Focus on how your breathing relaxes you.

4. Spread your arms out like airplane wings.

End every yoga session, and perhaps other relaxation techniques discussed in this book, with a sense of inner calm.

Quiet Mouse

1. Kneel on a mat with your knees and feet together. Your toes should point backward.

2. Lean back on your heels, sitting tall with your shoulders relaxed.

3. Breathing out slowly, lower your body until your head touches the floor.

4. Stretch your arms out in front of you.

5. Each time you breathe out, let your chest get closer to your knees.

6. Keeping your shoulders relaxed, take your arms back so that your hands are close to your feet.

Dead Man's Pose

1. Lie flat on your back with your knees bent.

2. Cross your arms over your chest.

3. Now breathe and stretch out your legs.

4. Let your arms flop down beside you, with your palms facing up. Let your body feel heavy on the floor, getting heavier every time you breathe out.

Chapter 7
Playing to Relax

Bullies, tests, insect bites, homework, chores, annoying little sisters—these are just some of the hundreds of little things that cause children to be stressed, but playing is one thing that always helps kids de-stress.

Play comes in all forms, from the peek-a-boo game played by infants to the one-on-one basketball game played by a twelve-year-old Michael Jordan wannabee. No matter how kids play, the simple act of playing produces biochemicals that directly interfere with the production of stress hormones, easing the mind away from everyday worries.

Of course, stress reduction is just one of the many benefits of play. Play is also an important way that your child learns about her world. Through the imaginative powers of play, she develops much of her language and intelligence and also explores her emotions. With play, she expresses her worries, conflicts, hopes, and fears. It is also an essential part of the way a child learns to relate to peers. Through play, your child will learn about sharing, taking turns, being patient, practicing good sportsmanship, playing fair, and much more.

Because play is such an important part of a child's emotional development, it is the primary medium through which counselors and other mental health professionals treat the emotional and behavioral problems of children under twelve. Anna Freud, the daughter of Sigmund Freud and a famous psychologist in her own right, once said that "play is the work of children," underscoring its prominence in every child's development.

All children play, just as naturally as they eat and breathe, so you may wonder why we bother to "prescribe" play as a way to relax. The answer is simple: play is under attack! Children simply don't play as much as they once did, largely due to advances in technology that have made electronic toys and computer games more attractive to children and cheaper for parents to buy. Go to any toy store and you'll see a large selection of computer games and video software for children as young as two. If you have young children at home, then you know that they would still rather play with trucks or dolls or blocks or puzzles, but by age seven, there is a significant shift away from traditional forms of play, despite its health and developmental benefits. A recent survey of how children use the Internet for play found that one social networking website for eight- to twelve-year-olds was so "sticky" that the average child who visited the site remained on it for two hours at a time. Two hours is a long time in a child's day, and when you add the two to three hours that American children typically spend watching TV, you can see that at an ever younger age, children are losing the opportunity to experience the joys and benefits of traditional play.

In this chapter, your child will find some time-honored ways to think about play and new ways to use play for relaxation and stress reduction. All forms of play reduce stress in children, but having a variety of play activities is best. Different kinds of play activities stimulate different areas of your child's intellectual, emotional, and social development, and all of these will help in coping with and overcoming stress.

"I'm bored!" Jason called to his mom, who was mopping the kitchen floor. "There's no one to play with and nothing to do. Today stinks."

Lots of kids sound like Jason at some time—even kids who have a house full of toys. What about you?

The truth is (as we're sure your parents have reminded you) that you have plenty of things to do, but your mind is just "stuck" for the moment. It's not about how many toys you have or think you need; it's all about how you use your imagination. Children in many parts of the world have very few toys, and many children have no toys at all. But still they find ways to play and have lots of fun with just things they find around their homes or their neighborhoods.

If you forget how many fun things you can do, we have a solution. It's called a No-More-Boredom Box. We guarantee that if you make a good box, you will always have something fun to do. The next page shows you how to make it.

No-More-Boredom Box

1. Ask your parents for a sturdy shoe box and twenty-five index cards.

2. With markers, write "No-More-Boredom Box" on the top of the box, and then color the sides.

3. Cut the index cards in half, and on each half card write down something fun to do. Think about all the ways you like to play, even ways you used to play when you were younger. You can even write down things you have never done but would like to try. If you need some help thinking of fifty activities, try brainstorming with a parent or friend.

4. Put the cards into the box, and also put in some small toys: a superball, some action figures or a small doll, a small puzzle, a pack of crayons and a small notebook. Look around and see what you can find. If you are like most kids, you have lots of small toys.

5. When you are bored (or even when you are not bored), shake the box around and reach in for a card or a toy. If you don't like the activity on the card (or maybe it is just impractical at the moment), you can have two more turns to pick, but no more than two.

6. Play for at least thirty minutes but not more than an entire day. (That's a joke!) Don't complain that you're bored or ask your parents what else you can do. Just have fun!

Do you like to play games? Most kids play all kind of games, like checkers, chess, Monopoly, miniature golf, bowling, and many more. But even though games are fun, and having fun is a way to get rid of stress, there is one problem that sometimes happens: if you are competitive or if you play games with people who hate to lose, then games can cause you stress.

That's not good, but there is a solution: you can play cooperative games, where everyone wins. Here is one of our favorite cooperative games.

Cooperative Air Hockey

You'll need one straw for each player, from three to seven small cups, a small wad of paper, and two poker chips. Without moving from their positions, players will try to blow the wad of paper around the cups and get it to the finish line. You'll find that it's very difficult to do this without cooperation!

1. Find from one to three other players and have everyone sit around a table.

2. Put the cups on the table upside down in a random pattern.

3. Use one chip as the starting point and the other as the finish line.

4. Put the small wad of paper by the starting point.

5. Working together, use the straws to blow the wad of paper to the finish line. Stay in position and don't move any of the cups.

6. If the wad of paper falls off the table, the game starts again.

7. When the wad of paper touches the finish line, the game is won.

Cooperative games are fun to play, and they teach you a good lesson too: some things just can't be done right without a little help from your friends.

Activity 37   My Relaxing Place

Have you ever built a house or a fort out of cushions or large cardboard boxes? We bet you have. Isn't it fun to crawl inside these special places and pretend that you are away from all of the rest of the world?

In this activity, you'll make a special place to relax, using couch cushions or large cardboard boxes, pillows, and a large bedsheet or two. You can use pieces of furniture, like a card table or a beanbag chair to help define your space. You can also use a tent or a playhouse if you have one at home. Your relaxing place will be a place you can go to when you are feeling worried or upset, or when you just want to chill out.

While you are there, you can imagine you are an animal—a fox or a squirrel or whatever animal you choose—safe in your den. How would you spend your time?

Keep some things you can use for calming activities in your relaxing place, such as books, puzzles, or a squeezable toy that helps you get rid of stress. Do not put in electronic toys of any kind. You can bring in an MP3 player or CD player, but remember that it is just for relaxing music.

The Cloud Maze

Do you like mazes? Here is a special maze that will remind you that breathing deeply from your belly will help you relax.

Take a pencil and place it on cloud number 1. Now move your pencil to each cloud in order from 1 to 10, circling each when you get to it. As your pencil circles each cloud, breathe in slowly and breathe out slowly.

When you are done with the maze, see if you feel more relaxed.

The Relaxation & Stress Reduction Workbook for Kids

Over and Over Again

Activity 39

Did you know that repetitive motion—doing the same action over and over again—causes your brain to produce chemicals that will help you relax? That's why kids (and even grown-ups) like to rock in rocking chairs, swing in hammocks, or even rock back and forth on their feet.

Lots of fun activities involve repetitive motion, and kids find them very relaxing when they are stressed. Here's a list of some of those activities. Circle the ones you like to do.

Playing with a yo-yo	Throwing a ball against a wall
Knitting	Swinging
Walking	Running
Seesawing	Doing needlepoint
Using a hula hoop	Rolling out dough or clay

Can you think of other kinds of repetitive motion that are fun and make you feel relaxed? Write them here.

_____

_____

_____

_____

_____

Play That Lasts a Lifetime

Kids like to play different ways at different ages. Babies may be happy just banging a pot with a wooden spoon. Toddlers like to stack blocks, splash around in the water, and pour sand in and out of a bucket. You probably like to play many different ways now, but in a year or two, you might have different things that are fun for you to do.

But there is one type of play that kids can do for years and years: hobbies. Many kids continue to have the same hobbies when they become teenagers and even grown-ups.

Do you have a hobby? If not, you should think about taking one up. A hobby is a great way to relax and reduce your stress. It can involve your whole family and help you meet new friends. You can have a hobby for your entire life!

Below you will find a list of hobbies that kids like. Put a check mark next to hobbies that you already have, and put a star next to hobbies that you think you might enjoy sometime in the future. You can add your own ideas, too!

Collecting

☐ Coins

☐ Stamps

☐ Stuffed animals, action figures, or other toys

☐ Rocks

☐ Buttons

☐ Bugs

☐ Baseball cards or other cards

☐ _____

☐ _____

Crafts

☐ Sewing

☐ Knitting

☐ Woodworking

☐ Beading

☐ _____

☐ _____

☐ _____

☐ _____

Arts

☐ Sculpting

☐ Drawing

☐ Painting

☐ Photography

☐ Writing

☐ _____

☐ _____

☐ _____

☐ _____

Performing

☐ Magic

☐ Dance

☐ Playing a musical instrument

☐ Acting

☐ _____

☐ _____

☐ _____

☐ _____

Other Hobbies

☐ Cooking

☐ Studying animals

☐ Inventing things

☐ _____

☐ _____

☐ _____

☐ _____

Hobbies are fun to do, and they are also fun to learn about. You can learn about your hobby on the Internet, read books in the library, and talk to friends and family members who have the same hobby.

Chapter 8
Relaxing Through Art

Art has an almost magic quality of being able to contain the powerful emotions that are triggered by a trauma without burying them. It is part of the therapy for children in many hospitals, foster homes, and shelters, and it is just as effective in less dramatic situations to help children deal with everyday stress.

It is hard to pinpoint exactly why art techniques are so useful, but there are no doubt a number of psychological principles at work. First, there is the emotional release inherent in the creative process. Art provides children with a medium for emotional discharge that can bring almost immediate relief. Just ask a child to draw a picture of his least favorite teacher or classmate with her head in the toilet and you'll see what we mean.

Psychologists also point out that art is a way of gaining symbolic control over problems that might normally be overwhelming. In a drawing, a child might portray himself as a superhero and the school bully as a slithering, frightened snake. Art fuels a child's imagination to help him develop a sense of mastery.

Children naturally gravitate toward art, as toward play, as a way to reduce their stress. You have only to go to a restaurant that hands out crayons and paper to children to see how quickly they use art to deal with the stress of waiting for their dinner.

Choose a place in your home that will not add stress to your life. Many parents prefer the kitchen table for art activities, since it is easier to clean up. Certainly it should not be a place where you will be concerned about getting art materials on your fabrics or rugs. Even though you should always use washable materials, worrying about making a mess will work against your efforts to use art as a way of opening up new channels of communication. Make sure your child has a large enough surface to work on. While working on the kitchen table, he should not have to worry about knocking over a vase or a sugar bowl.

Children can spontaneously do many of the activities in this section, particularly if materials like these are in easy reach:

- Crayons, oil pastels, and markers

- Tempera paint and watercolors

- Containers for paint and water

- Paper towels or rags

- Foam and bristle brushes of various sizes

- Materials for decoration, including yarn, buttons, beads, old costume jewelry, feathers, sequins, pieces of fabric, stickers, glitter, gauze, cotton balls, straws, pipe cleaners, and objects from nature (acorns, pebbles, dried berries, etc.)

- Old greeting cards, wrapping paper, construction paper, colored tissue paper, large drawing paper, heavy paper (90 lb.), brown paper bags, and newsprint

- Ruler

- Hole punch

- Safety scissors

- White glue, glue sticks, fabric glue, and tape

- Play dough, polymer clay, and hardening clay

Having these materials readily available will encourage your child to work in different art mediums, which in turn supports different emotional experiences. You can use several boxes and assign a "home" for it all, with one designated spot for paper of different sizes and types. Small clear boxes or zip-lock bags can hold objects like sequins, feathers, pom-poms, or other interesting little things you find. Remember to make cleaning up and putting things away when the child is finished a regular part of the process. This will certainly reduce stress for you! And if you don't have one already, designate a place to showcase your child's art. You'll both be regularly reminded of how special art can be.

Materials

- Old socks (clean ones!)

- Buttons

- Fabric glue

- Fabric marker

- Small pieces of felt in different colors

- Small items to make your puppet look interesting; for example, feathers, sequins, pipe cleaners, pom-poms, shapes cut out of felt or foam, yarn or string

Puppets are a lot of fun to make and to play with. They are also great for helping you work out worries, problems, and mixed-up feelings. For example, imagine you are moving to a new neighborhood or a new school. How will you meet new friends? What can you say to them? You could use sock puppets to put on a play of how you would like it to go. Or you could make up a really silly story about the craziest thing that could happen when you meet new kids. Looking at things in a funny way will help you feel less worried, too. You can also make one of your bad dreams into a sock puppet and talk back to it. Tell it just what you think about its scaring you. You'll see you are a lot bigger than your dream! Making sock puppets is also a fun thing to do with a couple of friends—or even your little sister or brother.

1. Put your hand inside the sock to decide where the eyes should be as you are working the mouth. Glue on buttons or circles cut from the felt for the eyes.

2. Use a fabric marker to draw in a mouth.

3. You can use pieces of string or yarn for hair or eyebrows. You can bend pipe cleaners into the shape of glasses and glue them on. Can you think of anything else?

4. Be sure to let the glue dry completely before playing with your new toy.

5. Have fun!

Activity 42   Sand Garden

Materials

- The top from a shoe box or a large foam tray, like the kind meat comes in

- Sand or dried grain, such as bulgur, millet, couscous, or small birdseed

- Small rocks in a variety of shapes and colors

- A popsicle stick or found branch to use as a rake

A sand garden can help you feel more peaceful and focused when you are worried or stressed, especially if you do your belly breathing before you start to play. The more you play with your garden, the more it will work for you. It is also a great way to play by yourself.

1. Fill your shoe box top or foam tray halfway up the side with sand or grain.

2. Make a tool to use as a rake for moving the sand around. It can be as simple as a popsicle stick or the end of a branch that you find already broken, or you can dream up something else.

3. Choose rocks from a special place you visited or any place you love. You can add other special objects to your garden, but don't use too many; keep your garden simple. Use an odd number of objects, because artists usually don't like things to be too balanced.

4. Use the tool to move the sand around the object.

5. You are the keeper of the sand garden, so you decide what goes in and what stays out.

Note to Parents

This activity is best for children six and older. Children under twelve will need adult supervision.

Materials

- One four-foot length of sixteen-gauge copper wire for each person. You can get this from any hardware store.

- Small objects that you make or find to show what you love. For example, if you play basketball, make a little toy basketball; if you love the beach, collect some small shells.

- Scraps of fabric

- Fabric glue

Imagine that you are a one-of-a-kind superhero, and people cheer when they see you. What would you be like? You might be a hero who does magic tricks or loves to make people laugh. Maybe you run like a cheetah or love basketball. Maybe you have a big heart and are a great friend.

Think of a time when you had to do something that was really hard but you grew brave and did it anyway. Think of something that is special about you or something you do really well. Then choose one or two things about you and show them to the world as you bend copper wire to create super you!

1. Hold the wire near the middle and form your head by making a loop about the size of quarter.

2. Use both ends of the wire to form yourself in an action pose. It may take awhile to get it just like you want it.

3. After you bend your body into shape, glue the small objects you made or found to your figure. These objects will add interesting details and give clues about who you are. For example, if you love to sing, add a little microphone made out of aluminum foil and string. Add sequins to show your sparkle, or make a skateboard or a magic wand. The sky's the limit!

Materials

- Pencil

- Scrap paper

- Drawing paper

- Oil pastels or crayons

- Old newspaper to put under your paper when you color

Do you ever doodle? You really don't have to use your noodle when you doodle, so it's a good way to relax and let go of your cares, but the pictures that you draw may also have some meaning to you. Like dreams, doodles can remind you of things and feelings that you may have forgotten.

1. On a piece of scrap paper, doodle some simple shapes, like circles, ovals, squares, triangles, and rectangles. If your feelings had a shape right now, what shape would they be? Could some shapes stand for something you love, like a person, a place, or even an animal? See which shapes feel right to you.

2. When you get some shapes you like, take a new piece of paper and repeat your doodle all over it in a pattern. The shapes can sometimes be small and sometimes large. They can connect with each other or overlap. Keep doing the feelings doodles over and over until you fill up your paper to the very edges.

3. Color it in.

It's fun, isn't it?

Activity 45　　　　　Memory Beads

Materials

- Beads in several different sizes, shapes, and colors

- Stretchy plastic string (You can get both the beads and string at any craft shop.)

- A couple of small bowls to hold the beads

- Ruler

- Scissors

Memory beads can help you remember good times and people you love who might not be with you all the time. Maybe your grandma has been visiting from another city and it's time for her to go home. Maybe your best friend is moving away and you are sad. Maybe you live mostly with one parent and don't see the other one as much.

You can make a bracelet for yourself or to give to the person you want to remember. Each bead can stand for a different memory of being together or for something you like about that person.

1. Think of things about the person you want to remember, like things that make you both laugh, things you are grateful for, good times you've had together, or favorite foods you've shared.

2. Choose a bead for each of these things. Use at least four or five beads on a bracelet, depending on the size of the beads.

3. Cut a six-inch length of stretchy string. If you'd rather make a necklace, cut a twelve-inch length.

4. Tie a knot on one end of the string so your beads will stay on.

5. String your beads.

6. Check for size around your neck or wrist. When it is right, tie the ends of the string together.

If you are giving these beads as a gift, you can make a memory card to go with it that explains each bead.

Activity 46

Relaxation Jar

Materials

- Small pieces of paper

- Pen or pencil

- Large, clean empty jar with a lid

- Inexpensive paintbrush

- Sheets of tissue paper of different colors or old magazine pages

- White glue

- Acrylic paint and a second paintbrush (if you want to paint the lid)

In this activity, you'll transform an ordinary jar into a magic relaxation jar that will look cool when it's done. In it, you'll put ideas for different things you can do when you are stressed. Use some of the stress-busting activities in this book, and maybe Mom or Dad can help you if you need more ideas. Here are some examples:

- Run up and down the stairs twenty times without stopping.

- Cuddle with my pet cat.

- Go outside and shoot baskets.

The Relaxation & Stress Reduction Workbook for Kids

1. Write your ideas on slips of paper. Try to include at least five special ideas that are all your own.

2. Prepare your paper pieces. If you are using old magazine pages, choose one or two colors. Cut them out in larger and smaller rectangles and squares. If you find some pictures of things that are relaxing to you, use those, too! If you are using tissue paper, you can tear it into larger and smaller strips or cut it into rectangles and other shapes of various sizes.

3. Starting at the top, use the brush to spread some glue on a small section of the jar. Lay the pieces of paper on the jar, one at a time. They will overlap, which is fine. Make sure you cover every bit of glass. When you get toward the bottom, turn the jar upside down and cover that surface. Let it dry completely. You can paint the lid with acrylic paint if you want.

4. Fill up your relaxation jar with your stress-busting ideas and keep it in a handy place.

It's ready to use anytime!

Activity 47   Musical String Drawing

Materials

- CD of soft, relaxing music

- CD player

- Four-foot length of yarn or thick string

- Sheet of old newspaper

- Large sheet of drawing paper

- Pencil

- Oil pastels

You listen to music with your ears, but what would relaxing music look like if it came through your body and out your hand as you listened? In this activity, you'll find out. Musical string drawing is even more fun when you do it with a bunch of people, so your whole family can do this—even your little brother or sister!

1. Turn on your relaxing music and do a little belly breathing for a minute or two. Then get your arm warmed up by taking an oil pastel and slowly making big, loopy lines all over your sheet of newspaper. Let your hand move in a large, loose way.

2. Now that you are warmed up, take a four-foot piece of yarn or string and play around with it on your drawing paper.

3. Arrange the string as a line that looks like the way the music sounds. Have the line of yarn begin and end by touching edges of the paper. Have it cross over itself a few times.

4. When it feels and looks right to you, trace the path of the string so that you can lift it up and still see where it was. Do one little piece at a time. Now you have your music on paper as a looping line.

5. Stop the music and use your oil pastels to color in the shapes. How are you going to use your colors? Will you use favorites or the colors of your feelings right now? You could have your colors move from darker to brighter to lighter across the page. It's up to you.

Chapter 9
Laugh to Relax, Then Laugh Some More

Your tire went flat on the highway. You got a call from the school nurse saying that your child got gum in her hair. The family dog got loose and pooped on your neighbor's morning paper. And it's only 10 a.m.! When everyday stress is the problem, laughter can help. Even when serious or chronic problems weigh you down, laughter can still help.

Scientists tell us that laughter is a magic elixir for the mind's troubles as well as the body's ills. In fact, laughter has the exact opposite effect on the body and mind as stress. Laughing lowers your blood pressure, lightens your mood, strengthens your immune system, and helps your body heal faster. Laughter has been accepted by the mainstream medical establishment as an important part of the recovery process from serious illness, and many hospitals have clowns and humor carts tour the wards, bringing mirth to otherwise difficult days.

Laughter is also a social lubricant, particularly for children. One study of children ages three through eighteen asked: "What are three things you like about your friends?" The phrase "likes to laugh and have fun" appeared in the responses from every age group. This finding adds another layer to the importance of humor and laughter in reducing stress, because peer interaction is an important stress reducer, while social isolation is one of the most significant stresses of childhood.

There are three general categories of humor: verbal, written, and visual. Within these categories, there are many ways to express humor.

- Verbal humor: jokes, puns, quips, stories, and anecdotes

- Written humor: books, comics, cartoons, and limericks

- Visual humor: movies, sight gags, mimes, clowns, and tricks

We're sure that you can find many ways to emphasize humor in your child's life, and the activities in this chapter should stimulate your thinking.

Making Fun of Stress

Making fun of the things that stress you can be funny, and it's also a good way to reduce your stress. We filled in some sentences to get you started.

- I know I'm *really* stressed when I step in dog poop and I'm too tired to clean it off my shoe.

- I know I'm *really* stressed when I put ketchup on my ice cream.

- I know I'm *really* stressed when I'm talking on the phone, and the person on the other end has already hung up.

- I know I'm *really* stressed when I put my socks on over my shoes.

Now you try it:

I know I'm *really* stressed when _____.

I know I'm *really* stressed when _____.

I know I'm *really* stressed when _____.

I know I'm *really* stressed when _____.

I know I'm *really* stressed when _____.

This is a fun activity for the whole family. Begin by taking several photo albums or boxes of photos and putting them on a table. Ask family members to pick out the funniest photo of themselves and pass it to the person on their right. Make a copy of the thought and speech balloons below, cut one out, and write in something funny that the person in the photograph might be saying or thinking. You can also do this on the computer. Most clip art programs have thought and speech balloons you can print out to use with your photos.

Activity 50   Joke Night

Do you know any good jokes? What do you think of these?

> *Knock, knock.*
>
> Who's there?
>
> *Leena.*
>
> Leena who?
>
> *Leena little closer and I'll tell you.*

> What time is it when ten elephants are chasing you?
>
> Ten after one.

> What do lazy dogs for fun?
>
> Chase parked cars.

Did these jokes makes you laugh? Did they make you groan? Did they make you run screaming from the house? It doesn't really matter, as long as they made you smile. Telling jokes is a great way to relax and also a great way to entertain your friends and family.

Are you good at remembering jokes? If the answer is no, you are not alone. Most people say that they can't remember jokes they were told just a few minutes earlier. But there is an easy solution. There are many great books for kids in the local library or bookstore, with hundreds of jokes you can read or memorize. You can also find great joke sites for kids on the Internet, but don't forget to ask your parents' permission

The Relaxation & Stress Reduction Workbook for Kids

before you check them out. We got the jokes at the beginning of this activity from www.azkidsnet.com, which has hundreds of jokes submitted by kids. You can also visit www.jokesbykids.com.

Even if you don't feel like sharing your jokes, you will enjoy reading them to yourself. Or why not get the whole family involved? Everyone can be a jokester. Here is how you can start a Family Joke Night:

1. Choose one night a week for Family Joke Night. Friday nights are usually good because everyone needs to relax after a week of work or school.

2. When dinner is over, each family member should tell a joke. You can use a joke book or have a joke written out that you want to read.

3. Have family members vote on who tells the best joke.

4. That person gets to choose dessert for the next Family Joke Night!

Activity 51   Crazy Dress Up

Some of the first things we laugh at when we are little are things that don't belong together. If a toddler sees his dad put his shoe on his head, he may think this is hysterical. If you see a friend who is a boy pretend to walk into a bathroom for girls and women, you may crack up.

In this game, you may get a lot of surprises as family members try on clothes that don't belong to them.

1. Ask all the family members to get five articles of old clothing and put them in a pile in the middle of the room.

2. As all the family members stand around the pile of clothing, blindfold one at a time and have that person pick out five articles of clothing.

3. When everyone has a pile of clothing, put on some music while each family member puts on all five pieces of clothing.

4. Have each family member "walk the runaway" and show off his or her new fashions.

Have a digital camera or video camera handy to capture these special moments. Perhaps you can submit them to a fashion magazine!

Some words just have a funny sound to them, like this bird name: "yellow-bellied sapsucker." Imagine calling your little brother that! Some plants also have funny names. We bet you've never climbed a bunya-bunya tree. The simple word "noodle" is also a funny word, don't you think? It's a lot of fun to use silly words in the middle of an otherwise ordinary story. This is especially fun to do with your whole family.

Copy our list of funny words onto index cards cut in quarters, and put them in a bag. Be sure to include your own funny words—we know you know some. Start by having each person take a word out of the bag.

Then the nutty story begins. The first person start by saying, "Once upon a time there was a...." After making up a couple of sentences, he has to use his funny word in the story. Then he puts his card back in the bag, and it is the next person's turn.

Remember that a story usually has a problem or big challenge in it. Keep going for a couple of rounds of silly words till the problem somehow gets fixed or something else crazy happens. Then give it an ending.

You can play this story game for fun on long car rides. We just hope that you can stop laughing before you wet your pants!

Funny Words

We used a couple of the words in sentences just to give you an idea—and because it was fun!

funny bone	belly button	baby toe
sour pickle	sweet potato	noodle

I was minding my own business, just practicing my belly breathing, when a giant noodle crawled up the street and wrapped itself around my funny bone!

goon	wandering tattler	lima bean
tufted titmouse	lousewart	yellow-bellied sapsucker

She was horrible to look upon, with hairy gray lousewarts growing out of her nose and ears.

loon	moon	kidney bean

He went to the hospital to have his kidney bean removed.

fortune cookie	stinky cheese	bumblebee

I had a nice plump bumblebee with my pudding at noontime. It gave me a real buzz.

blue-footed booby	muck	boojum tree
cuckoo	skunk cabbage	zucchini

Madame Zucchini will now read your fortune, but first you must cross her palm with a lima bean or two.

bunya-bunya	speckled trout

Imagine my surprise at finding a speckled trout in my breakfast cereal. I was just looking for the free toy inside the box.

Make-a-Face Photo Op

Everyone likes to make funny faces, but most of us have no idea what we look like. Now you can change all that. Using a digital camera, ask all of your family members or friends to make the silliest faces they can. Take a picture of each silly face. Make sure that someone uses the camera to take a picture of you, too!

Now transfer the digital photos onto your computer (get some help if you need it) and you can make any of the following with the faces:

- Playing cards

- Postage stamps

- A poster of all the different faces

- Greeting cards

- Stationery with the faces around the border

- A calendar

There are several websites on the Internet such as www.flickr.com and www.snapfish.com, that can turn photos into fun projects.

Activity 54   The Funny Place

Is there a place in your home where you can post things that you think are funny for other people to see? Maybe there is a cartoon or comic strip you like. What about a photograph from a newspaper or a magazine, or a joke, riddle, or short article from the paper?

Ask your parents to think of a good place where you can put funny things, like on the refrigerator or a bulletin board. Then ask everyone in the family to post something funny there at least once a week.

The Relaxation & Stress Reduction Workbook for Kids

Do you know what a prank is? It's a trick designed to fool someone. Some people play mean pranks on others, but that is not the kind of prank we are talking about. Mean pranks, which almost always get people mad at you, will not help you relax and may get you punished or yelled at.

The pranks that can help people laugh are funny, not mean or harmful. Here are some pranks that kids we know have played:

- Michael put salt in his hair before he went to the dinner table. He scratched and scratched his head and said, "My dandruff has really gotten bad." His mom was really upset to see all the fake dandruff, but then she smiled when she looked a little closer. And even though she thought the prank was funny, she still made him clean up the salt and wash his hair when dinner was over.

- Megan told her parents that she had found a good way to keep track of her chores by creating a chores chart. They were very pleased at the thought that their daughter had become so responsible. But when Megan handed the chart to her parents, this is what it said.

Monday: Scrub the toilet with the leftover turkey.

Tuesday: Take out the trash and then bring it back in.

Wednesday: Sleep all day so I don't have to make my bed.

Thursday: Wash the side window of the car.

Friday: Switch Dad's sock drawer with Mom's underwear drawer.

Saturday: Feed the dog our dinner, and we'll eat the dog's dinner.

Sunday: Make the bed while I'm still in it, and sleep all day.

Megan's parents thought that their daughter was funny and clever—but they made her do her regular chores anyway.

Gross pranks can be funny, too, at least most of the time. Sometimes kids get too gross—or make a huge mess—and then it isn't funny at all. Here are two ideas you can try to gross out your family and friends. If they look sick to their stomachs but still have smiles on their faces, then you have done a good job!

- Hide a few plastic bugs in your hand, then start to scratch your chest. Scratch and scratch under your shirt, then open your hand to reveal the nasty creatures. Ask your parents what they've been using for laundry detergent.

- Invite some friends over for a fun scavenger hunt. They'll probably think it's a regular scavenger hunt, where people search for things you can find in or around most homes. But when they arrive, tell them that it is actually a disgusting scavenger hunt, where you will search for … disgusting things, of course! Here are some things you can put on your scavenger hunt list. On the blank lines, add five more things that you think are gross.

Worms	Slime or mold
Dirty socks	Jar of mud

_____

_____

_____

_____

_____

Give each team of players a shoe box and a copy of the list. The first team that returns with all the disgusting things on the list wins the prize. What would be a good prize for this hunt? How about some fake vomit or fake dog poop? We emphasize the word "fake"!

Want more ideas for disgusting things to do? Pick up the book *Gross Me Out!* (2005, Lark Books), by Ralph Retcher and Betty Lou Poo (no joke!), which will tell you how to make poop soap, fake blood, and edible eyeballs. Several of the ideas in this activity were inspired by this book.

Appendix
More Ways to Relax and Reduce Stress

Aromatherapy

Aromatherapy is defined as the practice of using essential plant oils to stimulate psychological and physical well-being. It has been used in many diverse cultures for thousands of years. Practitioners of aromatherapy believe that natural oils must be used and that the popular scented candles and other products are not really beneficial. Lavender, eucalyptus, and geranium are among the many plant oils that are supposed to aid in relaxation. While there is no clear scientific evidence that aromatherapy works, there is certainly enough anecdotal and historic use to make this a technique worth exploring.

Biofeedback

Biofeedback involves using the conscious mind to mechanically monitor body functions. There are all sorts of apparatuses that can measure these functions and give people visual or auditory feedback. In the case of stress reduction, the most common function measured is called the *galvanic sweat response* (GSR), a measurement of the minute changes in the sweat glands that are affected by stress. Instruments that measure GSR are relatively inexpensive and can be bought for under $100. This can be a useful technique in helping children who are mechanically minded and might be less inclined to show interest in techniques like yoga or guided imagery.

Diet

A healthy diet, with a balance of protein, whole grains, fruits, and vegetables, is considered the best way to stimulate the brain chemicals that fight off stress. We also know that drinks and foods high in sugar and caffeine, common in the diets of many kids, should be avoided. Processed foods and foods with certain additives are also thought to trigger stress reactions in the body, which may be particularly harmful to children with ADHD and other behavioral disorders. Foods high in tryptophan (like turkey or milk) can help calm and relax the body, and foods high in antioxidants (such as blueberries and leafy green vegetables) will help the body fight stress and disease.

Music

Music has a powerful and immediate effect on the brain. Loud music or music with a harsh beat is very stressful, even though kids may enjoy it. There is particular concern that the amplification of music through earphones attached to iPods and other MP3 players may cause physical damage as well as undue stress. On the other hand, relaxing music, whether it is classical or contemporary, slows the body down, lowering blood pressure and reducing the heart rate. One composer, Gary Lamb (www.garylamb.com), has composed music to the beat of the human heart, which has been used in clinics and schools to relax children.

Nature

As Richard Louv says in his book *Last Child in the Woods: Saving Our Children from Nature-Deficit Disorder* (2008, Algonquin Books), most of today's children are missing out on the therapeutic benefits of being close to nature, and this lack may be particularly detrimental to children with emotional and behavioral disorders. Nature is all around us, not just at national parks or at summer camps. Taking time to experience nature every day will have benefits for the whole family.

Pet Therapy

Virtually any pet, even a goldfish, seems to help in relaxation and stress reduction. Animal-assisted therapy has been used with children who have a wide range of disorders, from anger-control problems to autism, and seems to aid in stress reduction as well as socialization. Without proper supervision, of course, household pets can add to stress. If you are thinking of getting a pet for your child, make sure that you consider the well-being of the animal as well as the pleasure and benefits it will bring your family.

Conclusion

Now that you have read this workbook, you know that there are many ways to relax, and you know how important relaxation is, too. Taking just ten to fifteen minutes to relax each and every day will put you in a better mood and help protect you from the bad effects of all that nasty stress in your life. You also know that relaxation activities are easy to do. Just do some belly breathing or some yoga or some fun art or play activities. Tell some jokes and laugh a little!

So can you do this every day? You can! Taking time to relax is a habit you need to develop, just like brushing your teeth or washing your hands before a meal. You don't even think about those positive habits; you just do them because they are important, and that is the way you need to think about relaxation activities.

Here is your challenge. See if you can have everyone in the family do at least one relaxation activity every day for a month. Try to do it at the same time each day, and keep track of what you do on a calendar. If you can remember to take time to relax every day for a month, then you can do this every day for the rest of your life. And we guarantee that all your days will be happier and healthier.

Lawrence E. Shapiro, Ph.D., is a nationally recognized child psychologist who is known for his innovative play-oriented techniques. He has written over two dozen books and created over forty therapeutic games. Shapiro is founder of the Childswork/Childsplay catalog and publishing company, a leading distributor of psychologically oriented toys and games. He is author of numerous books, including *How to Raise a Child with a High EQ* and *An Ounce of Prevention*. He lives in Norwalk, CT.

Robin K. Sprague, LCPC, is a licensed clinical professional counselor in Bangor, ME. She holds a master's degree from Boston College. For over twenty years, she has worked in the field of human services. Her specialty is helping children successfully transition through difficult life challenges in order to prevent future psychological problems, especially anxiety disorders. A highly creative person herself, Sprague enjoys painting, writing, and laughing out loud.

Foreword writer **Matthew McKay, Ph.D.**, is a professor at the Wright Institute in Berkeley, CA. He has authored and coauthored numerous books, including *The Relaxation and Stress Reduction Workbook, Self-Esteem, Thoughts and Feelings, When Anger Hurts*, and *ACT on Life Not on Anger*.

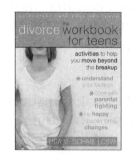